DATE DUE

DEC 0 5 2007		
NOV 1 4 2008		
NOV 1 7 2010		

Plant Nutrition

The Green World

Ethnobotany

Forestry

Horticulture

Photosynthesis and Respiration

Plant Biotechnology

Plant Cells and Tissues

Plant Development

Plant Diversity

Plant Ecology

Plant Genetics

Plant Nutrition

Plant Nutrition

Alex C. Wiedenhoeft

Series Editor
William G. Hopkins
Professor Emeritus of Biology
University of Western Ontario

CHELSEA HOUSE
PUBLISHERS
An imprint of Infobase Publishing

Plant Nutrition

Copyright © 2006 by Infobase Publishing

Chelsea House
An imprint of Infobase Publishing
132 West 31st Street
New York NY 10001

Library of Congress Cataloging-in-Publication Data

Wiedenhoeft, Alex C.
   Plant nutrition / Alex C. Wiedenhoeft.
      p. cm. — (The green world)
Includes bibliographical references.
ISBN 0-7910-8564-3
1. Plants—Nutrition—Juvenile literature. I. Title. II. Green world (Philadelphia, Pa.).
QK867.W54 2006
572'.42—dc22   2005032187

Text and cover design by Keith Trego

Printed in the United States of America

Bang 21C 10 9 8 7 6 5 4 3 2 1

This book is printed on acid-free paper.

Table of Contents

Introduction

By William G. Hopkins

"Have you thanked a green plant today?" reads a popular bumper sticker. Indeed, we should thank green plants for providing the food we eat, fiber for the clothing we wear, wood for building our houses, and the oxygen we breathe. Without plants, humans and other animals simply could not exist. Psychologists tell us that plants also provide a sense of well-being and peace of mind, which is why we preserve forested parks in our cities, surround our homes with gardens, and install plants and flowers in our homes and workplaces. Gifts of flowers are the most popular way to acknowledge weddings, funerals, and other events of passage. Gardening is one of the fastest-growing hobbies in North America and the production of ornamental plants contributes billions of dollars annually to the economy.

Human history has been strongly influenced by plants. The rise of agriculture in the Fertile Crescent of Mesopotamia brought previously scattered hunter-gatherers together into villages. Ever since, the availability of land and water for cultivating plants has been a major factor in determining the location of human settlements. World exploration and discovery was driven by the search for herbs and spices. The cultivation of New World crops—sugar, cotton, and tobacco—was responsible for the introduction of slavery to America, the human and social consequences of which are still with us. The push westward by English colonists into the rich lands of the Ohio River Valley in the mid-1700s was driven by the need to increase corn production and was a factor in precipitating the French and Indian War. The Irish Potato Famine in 1847 set in motion a wave of migration, mostly to North America, that would reduce the population of Ireland by half over the next 50 years.

I can recall as a young university instructor directing biology tutorials in a classroom that looked out over a wooded area, I would ask each group of students to look out the window and tell me what they saw. More often than not, the question would be met with a blank, questioning look. Plants are so much a part of our environment and the fabric of our everyday lives that they rarely register in our conscious thought. Yet today, faced with disappearing rainforests, exploding population growth, urban sprawl, and concerns about climate change, the productive capacity of global agricultural and forestry ecosystems is put under increasing pressure. Understanding plants is even more essential as we attempt to build a sustainable environment for the future.

THE GREEN WORLD series opens doors to the world of plants. This series describes what plants are, what plants do, and where plants fit into the overall circle of life. In this book, you will learn about the nutrients that plants require and how they obtain them, the intimate relationship between plant roots and soils, and how plant nutrition affects the nutritional quality of the food you eat.

William G. Hopkins
Professor Emeritus of Biology
University of Western Ontario

1 Introduction to Plants and Plant Nutrition

I believe a leaf of grass is no less than the journey-work of the stars.

— Walt Whitman

Introduction to Plants and Plant Nutrition

SALLY'S SCIENCE FAIR PROJECT

When Sally's biology teacher told her class that they must perform long-term experiments for this year's science fair, she was elated. Even though it was only a few weeks into the school year, Sally's teacher had been focusing on plants as the first part of the class, and Sally loved plants. Her family lived on a farm in the country, where her dad grew soybeans, feed corn, and hay for their beef cattle. They also had a large garden for growing their family's food, and Sally earned part of her allowance by helping in the garden.

Based on her practical experience on the farm and in the garden, Sally was not surprised when her teacher began to talk about the obvious requirements for plant growth: water, light, and air. When her teacher spoke about other requirements of plants—essential mineral nutrients—she was intrigued. She knew that her dad spread fertilizer on their fields and she had, much to her dismay, helped to add manure to their home garden and till it into the soil. She had never really considered the scientific basis for these farming practices and thought that a science fair project about plant nutrition could teach her more.

After class that day, Sally talked to her teacher about doing some basic experiments on the nutritional requirements of plants. After some research in the library and consultation with her teacher, Sally decided to test the effects of different kinds of soil, different watering regimes, and the requirement for light, water, and air. She went home that night with a lot of work before her.

THE PLANT WAY OF LIFE

Plants, via **photosynthesis**, are the providers of energy for virtually all of the terrestrial organisms in the world. Photosynthesis, performed by plants, is the critical step in energy conversion from the sun, taking carbon dioxide from the air and using water and light to make sugar, which is the basic building block or starting material for all **organic** matter. The breakfast you ate today, whether eggs, cereal, or bacon, was derived, ultimately, from plants. Plants also produced the raw materials for the clothes you are wearing, whether cotton, polyester, or leather. The home in which you live is likely constructed with plant materials, and the page on which these words are printed is formed largely of plant matter. Plants are the world's air conditioning systems, the purifiers of streams and rivers throughout the world, the primary generators of atmospheric oxygen, and the storage providers of over 90% of the world's terrestrial biomass. Plants are the single most important group of terrestrial organisms for energy capture from the sun, and the vast majority of all terrestrial organisms depend on plants for food, shelter, or both.

Most terrestrial life is dependent on plants and their ability to form organic compounds from inorganic constituents. To accomplish this, plants require chemicals called **essential nutrients** to carry out photosynthesis, and thus produce energy. Though photosynthesis is a marvel, both biochemically and energetically, it also comes with certain costs in terms of the lifestyle that terrestrial plants can successfully pursue. To survive and reproduce, plants require water, air, light, and relatively small amounts of other nutrients. Furthermore, plants are **sessile** organisms: they grow in one place and cannot move about freely. This is in stark contrast to an animal that might scamper off to a new location if its current habitat becomes uncomfortable or undesirable. The only way a rooted plant can move is to grow into a new position, and the process of growth requires the expenditure of energy. To live in a single location in some cases for thousands of years and gain all the necessities for life is one of the great challenges that plants face.

ENERGY CAPTURE AND NUTRITION

Every plant growing in the world is engaged in a slow but bitter struggle to overcome the limits of its circumstances and make a living from light, water, air, and small but critical amounts of minerals from the soil. Biologists break organisms into two broad categories on the basis of how they secure their food. There are those organisms that eat other living or once living creatures and plants; these are called **heterotrophs.** Heterotrophs include animals, **fungi,** most **bacteria,** and most **protists.** The other group, called **autotrophs,** is made up of organisms that are able to produce their own food using energy from some other source, such as light or higher energy sulfur compounds. They include plants, algae, cyanobacteria, purple sulfur bacteria, and relatively few others. Autotrophs can be separated into two smaller groups: **chemoautotrophs** and **photoautotrophs.** Chemoautotrophs produce their food using chemical energy, and photoautotrophs produce their food using light energy.

In the case of virtually all life on Earth, the fundamental building block is the chemical element carbon. Carbon compounds are also the primary energy source for heterotrophs. Carbon occurs naturally in the environment as carbon dioxide, but this form of carbon is not usable by heterotrophs, because there is very little energy stored in carbon in this form. Autotrophs, however, readily use carbon dioxide because they have the mechanisms for elevating its energy level. Although heterotrophs cannot use carbon dioxide, they must use high-energy carbon compounds produced by autotrophs.

CHEMICAL CONSTITUENTS OF THE PLANT BODY

Photosynthesis, either directly or indirectly, consumes the vast bulk of the water transported throughout a plant, but water and its component elements are not generally considered plant nutrients. Furthermore, though 90% of the dry weight of a plant is made of carbon and oxygen, neither the carbon nor the oxygen of carbon dioxide are considered plant nutrients. Given that these elements—carbon, oxygen, and hydrogen—make up the vast bulk of the dry weight of a plant, what elements are left and why are they important if they occur in such small amounts in the plant body? The full answers to these questions will unfold in subsequent chapters, but in short, the relative prevalence of an element is not necessarily indicative of its importance in plant biology. In some cases, the lack of even tiny amounts of a mineral can have significant negative impacts on the growth and life cycle of a plant.

ESSENTIAL NUTRIENTS

There are some 240,000 species of higher plants and not all of those species will have the same mineral needs, at the same scale. Some will require a specific element in much higher concentration than others, and others will be able to tolerate a much higher concentration of an essential element that would, to a different species, be toxic. Such variability is inherent in biology, and for this reason most generalities, such as the definition of an essential nutrient, need to have some wiggle room in interpretation.

Nutrient deficiencies in plants are often made most evident by plant physiological responses that can be readily observed (Figure 1.1). Such a response is called a **symptom**. Nutrient deficiency symptoms tend to occur in three major patterns: localized to the younger tissues, localized to the more mature tissues, or widely distributed across the plant. In each case, the distribution of the symptoms can help a person determine the nature of the deficiency experienced by the plant or, if the deficient nutrient is already known, make an inference about the role the nutrient plays in the plant body.

For example, in the case of deficiencies that result in symptoms in the youngest parts of the plant, one can infer that the nutrient in question is not easily mobile within the plant, and thus reserves of the nutrient cannot be easily translocated to the areas of need. This inference is sound because plants almost always strive to protect and provide for their youngest tissues and the structures that give rise to them. Thus, if it were possible for the plant to move the nutrient to the young tissue, it would almost

Figure 1.1 Nutrient deficiencies in plants are caused by a lack of mineral nutrients. The growing seedling (center right) does not have enough room in its pot to absorb nutrients and is suffering from excessive use of fertilizer. The fertilizer has caused the green leaves to curl under (top left). Nitrogen deficient leaves have turned pale yellow in color, phosphorus deficient leaves curled and turned purplish in color (lower left), and potassium deficient leaves developed bronze edges (bottom right).

certainly do so. Conversely, if the symptoms of deficiency first appear in more mature tissues, it is reasonable to infer that the nutrient in question is highly mobile and the plant, always seeking to protect its young tissues, sacrifices the health of the older tissue to protect the young, growing organs. Evenly distributed symptoms can imply that the lack of the nutrient is widespread and systemic, that it functions in a general role equally throughout the plant body, or that it affects the health and vigor of the plant at a large scale.

Common Symptoms of Nutrient Deficiencies

A common symptom of nutrient deficiency is **chlorosis**, the yellowing of the leaves and other green parts of the plant (Figure 1.2). Often, chlorosis is first evident in the spaces of the leaves between the **veins**, and then spreads to the veins. In extreme cases, the entire leaf will become yellow and eventually the plant may drop the affected leaf in a process called leaf **abscission**.

Another common symptom of some nutrient deficiencies is an **etiolated** growth habit. This results in tall, spindly plants with few leaves and a high degree of **internodal** elongation. This symptom is also typical of plants that are grown in the dark, forced to rely on stored energy from the seed or roots until the plant can reach sun again. A similar pattern can be seen in plants that are deprived of certain nutrients.

The converse of the tall, spindly habit of etiolated growth is the phenomenon of **stunted growth**. Stunted plants fail to develop normally and often have small leaves and very short or compressed internodes that result in apparent whorls of leaves, with no **stem** apparent between them. Stunted plants often have greatly reduced productivity and are not vigorous producers of flowers and fruits, if they form them at all.

A common and severe symptom of some nutrient deficiencies is **necrosis**, the formation of dead spots or lesions, often in the leaves, where the plant cannot sustain life any longer.

Figure 1.2 A common symptom of nutrient deficiency is chlorosis, the yellowing of leaves and other green parts of the plant. Chlorosis is first evident in the spaces of the leaves between the veins.

Necrotic lesions represent a major symptom of nutrient deficiency that cannot be amended by adding the missing nutrients. Once a leaf or a part of a leaf is dead, it cannot grow again. Many plants can, however, grow a new flush of leaves if the missing nutrient is added early enough in the growing season.

It is important to note that though these symptoms can be caused by nutrient deficiencies, there are many other stimuli that can result in the same symptoms. An insect **pest** infesting a plant could cause such symptoms, as can bacterial, fungal, or viral plant **pathogens**. Other stress conditions, such as drought or flooding, can also cause some of these symptoms. In fact, it is not uncommon for a plant experiencing nutrient or environmental stress to also become infested or infected as a result of its weakened condition. Rarely in the natural world will any particular symptom have just one cause. A concatenation of influences is likely to produce any symptoms seen, and only an expert with the plant species in question who is knowledgeable about the soil and other conditions of the location should make nutrition-related diagnoses without additional quantitative data from laboratory assays.

Nutrient Cycles

Nutrients, such as nitrogen, are moved through the world in cycles of ever increasing scale and complexity. For example, nitrogen in a tree may be moved to developing leaves in the spring, used there all growing season, and then mostly imported back into the stem for storage over winter. In the spring, it might be moved out to the new leaves again. This represents a simplified cycle within one tree. Not all of that nitrogen, however, was returned to the tree, and instead some remained in the leaf, which fell from the tree in the autumn. On the forest floor, bacteria and fungi colonized the leaf, and the nitrogen was incorporated into their bodies. In time they died, and some of the nitrogen was released to the soil, where it was taken up by the tree's roots, and thus it returned to the tree. This is a cycle between the tree and some of the other organisms in its environment.

Not all of the nitrogen made it into the soil to be taken up by the tree, however. Herbivorous mammals ate a few leaves and that nitrogen was incorporated into their **proteins**. Eventually these mammals excreted the nitrogen or eventually died, and **microbes** attacked either the droppings or the corpse. Some of the nitrogen was used as energy by special bacteria and the waste product of such bacteria is nitrogen gas. The nitrogen gas entered the atmosphere, where it may stay hundreds of years before it is again brought into a life cycle. Some of the nitrogen from the fallen leaf was washed away by rain, and eventually ended up in the ocean, where some of it will eventually form sediments on the ocean floor. Of the nitrogen in the atmosphere, some of it was returned to the terrestrial cycle by lightning, which makes plant-usable forms of nitrogen from nitrogen gas. Some of it was fixed into usable forms by human industrial processes. Specialized bacteria also contributed fixed nitrogen to the terrestrial cycle. Eventually, the nitrogen returns to plants in a usable form, and the cycle continues.

This is a highly simplified version of small portions of the global nitrogen cycle, and for each major plant nutrient, such a cycle can be devised. Depending on the nutrient in question, the details of the cycle can be very different. For example, the phosphorus cycle doesn't have a significant atmospheric component, but the aquatic component is prominent, and the return

A Cautionary Tale About Scientific Paradigms

As early as the 17th century, scientists studied the necessary components for growing and maintaining plants. While some aspects of plant nutrition and physiology had been known since the beginning of agriculture, such as the need for water, the specific roles played by these building blocks were unknown.

In a famous experiment conducted by the Belgian physician J.B. Van Helmont, a willow shoot weighing 5 pounds was placed in a measured quantity of soil, and then was watered daily with distilled water when rain water did not suffice to maintain the health of the plant. After five years, the willow plant weighed some 169 pounds and Van Helmont concluded that the 164 pounds gained by the plant must have come from the water that was added over the course of the experiment. Leonardo DaVinci carried out similar experiments, with the same conclusion being drawn. It would be roughly a century later that plant physiologists would show that plants also need the air for growth.

Van Helmont's experiment can serve as a cautionary tale for anyone studying science, or conducting his or her own experiments. According to the state of scientific knowledge in Van Helmont's day, it could not have been known that air is composed of different gases, each with distinct

of phosphorus to the biotic cycle relies heavily on geologic processes, rather than biological ones.

Summary

Plants are critical to life on Earth as we know it due to their ability to produce fixed carbon using photosynthesis. As a result of photosynthesis, plants have certain limitations and requirements, including the need for essential mineral elements. A lack of these elements can result in damage to the plant, or failure of the plant to grow or thrive. These critical nutrients move throughout nature in complex cycles that for some nutrients cross the entire Earth.

chemical properties and roles in biology. Thus, it can be argued that, though Van Helmont's conclusions were incorrect with respect to the source from which his plant gained weight, his reasoning and experimental methods were as precise and accurate as could be hoped for the time.

Van Helmont was limited in his experiments not by his own knowledge or intelligence, but rather by the scientific paradigm that was in effect at that time. The history of science is filled with such events; experiments that are as well designed as they can be, given the state of scientific understanding at the time. We can look back on these early works with both a smile and grave respect. Van Helmont came close to discovering critically important things about plant physiology. If he had measured the water added to his plant, and the water that evaporated from the leaves, he might have inferred that the weight of this plant had come from the air. His scientific paradigm, however, would likely have prevented him from correctly understanding the results of his experiment. It would take a revolution in scientific thought about chemistry, a scientific paradigm shift, for Van Helmont's results to be interpreted in a more modern way.

2 Macronutrients

Nature provides a free lunch,
but only if we control our appetites.
— William Ruckelshaus

Macronutrients

SALLY'S EXPERIMENTAL SETUP

After some consultation with her parents about what materials she could use from around the farm, Sally sat down to design her experiment. She had learned from her biology teacher and some textbooks that plants require certain nutrients in relatively high concentrations. She decided that she could easily test for this requirement. As she was planning her experiment, she decided how she would test the requirement for air, water, and light, in addition to the mineral requirements that were to be the basis of her experiments.

To record her data, Sally made a table. She had learned in previous science classes that all experiments had three main facets: variables, controls, and replication. Variables are the experimental conditions that are manipulated in each **treatment** being tested. Controls are experimental treatments designed to set and test the limits of the experimental design and show that each variable has been properly isolated from other variables.

After additional conversations with her teacher, Sally learned that there are two basic kinds of controls, positive and negative. A positive control is used to show that the experimental material, in this case, kidney bean seeds from a gardening store, is working properly. Negative controls limit the conditions of the experiment to show that a variable that appears necessary for the experiment is required.

Replication, she had learned, is an underappreciated but absolutely critical aspect of an experiment. It is nothing more than performing each experimental treatment several times to confirm that the experimental data are due to the treatments and not from random chance.

You can see from Sally's experimental table that she intends to test the requirements for air, light, and water, with both **positive** and **negative controls** in each case (Table 2.1). She also will look at the effects of three different kinds of soils and two different types of watering media on her plants.

Table 2.1 Sally's Experimental Table

	DARK, NO AIR			DARK, AIR			LIGHT, NO AIR			LIGHT, AIR		
	NO WATER	DISTILLED WATER	NUTRIENT SOLUTION	NO WATER	DISTILLED WATER	NUTRIENT SOLUTION	NO WATER	DISTILLED WATER	NUTRIENT SOLUTION	NO WATER	DISTILLED WATER	NUTRIENT SOLUTION
Autoclaved soil												
Washed sand												
Normal soil												
Autoclaved soil												
Washed sand												
Normal soil												
Autoclaved soil												
Washed sand												
Normal soil												

THE BASIC MACRONUTRIENTS

There are many essential plant nutrients, but they can be divided into two general groups based on the quantities of the nutrient needed for a healthy plant: the **macronutrients**, which are required in relatively large amounts, and the **micronutrients**, which are sometimes required in only trace amounts. This separation of macronutrients and micronutrients is a useful idea for tracking the importance of various minerals to plant nutrition, but it is an inherently artificial method of grouping the elements. There can be significant biological variability in the demand for various nutrients, so that while such categories of macronutrients and micronutrients are conceptually useful, they should not be considered hard and fast rules for the nutrition of every plant.

With those caveats, there are six basic macronutrients required by virtually all plants: nitrogen (N), phosphorus (P), potassium (K), sulfur (S), calcium (Ca), and magnesium (Mg). These are the main elements, apart from carbon (C), hydrogen (H), and oxygen (O), which are not considered plant nutrients. For each macronutrient, there is a set of properties that must be considered.

- The functions of the element in the plant

- The original sources of the element in the natural world (other than decaying matter from other organisms) and the nutrient's abundance or availability

- The forms of the nutrient available to the plant

- The likelihood of deficiency in a plant

- The specific effects of deficiency

Nitrogen (N)

Nitrogen is the most frequently limiting nutrient. Within the plant, nitrogen serves in the same ways it does in other organisms—as

Nutrient Solutions and the Artificiality of Experiments

Nutrient solutions are critical parts of plant nutrition research. By controlling what nutrients are added to an experimental plant, specific deficiencies can be caused in the plant, and the results of that deprivation can be seen. One of the easiest ways to conduct such an experiment is to use a hydroponic system. Hydroponics is the science of growing plants in liquid media, rather than in pots of soil. For a hydroponic solution to sustain plant growth, it must provide the required nutrients at appropriate concentrations, and in the correct forms that are available to the plant. Developing a useful hydroponic solution can be a time consuming process.

Different plant species may require nutrients in different concentrations, ratios, or chemical forms for efficient absorption. Most plant nutrient solutions, whether used in hydroponics or for watering plants in pots, often employ nutrients at much higher concentrations than they would find in natural soil. The main reason for this approach is to save time in the lab. For example, if there is a high concentration of nutrients present, the solution may need to be changed only once a week instead of once a day, saving considerable time, particularly in an experiment with 500 beakers of plants.

Of course, any time an experimental condition differs greatly from the condition found in nature, the results must be carefully assessed. The scientific method requires the isolation of variables and the control of all variables not being tested. Unfortunately, the natural world is not as easily manipulated as is a hydroponic beaker in a lab, so great care must be used when interpreting the results of an experiment. All experiments are by definition artificial, and must be treated as such. Meticulous reasoning about the relevance of an experimental result is as much the responsibility of a scientist as is a sound experimental design.

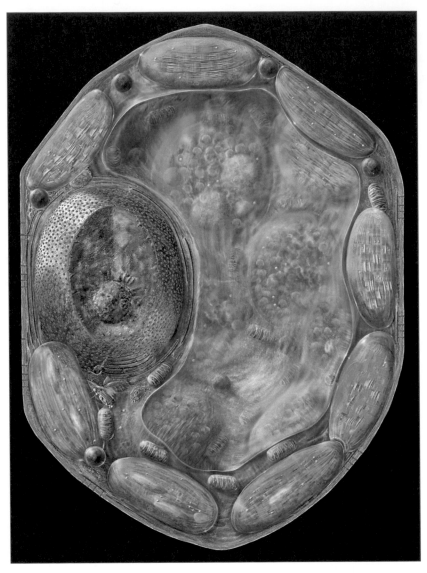

Figure 2.1 The features of a plant cell include the cell wall (yellow), the chloroplasts (green ovals circling the cell), a large central vacuole, the nucleus (pink, center left), and mitochondria (orange ovals).

a component of **amino acids** and **nucleic acids**. Nitrogen also plays a critical role in the structure of **chlorophyll**, the primary light harvesting compound of photosynthesis. This, along with its structural role in amino acids, explains why plants require large amounts of nitrogen, and thus why it is often the limiting nutrient for plant growth.

The largest natural source of nitrogen is the Earth's atmosphere, which is roughly 78% gaseous nitrogen, an inert and essentially biologically unavailable form of the element (Figure 2.1). Its biological unavailability is because the two nitrogen atoms form an extremely stable bond, which is not easily broken. Apart from human industrial processes that fix nitrogen gas to solid or liquid forms, the primary means of nitrogen **fixation** are through the high temperature and energy of lightning strikes and biological nitrogen fixation by bacteria. These processes produce nitrogen in three main forms, each of which are available to plants: nitrate, nitrite, and ammonium.

Nitrogen deficiency is commonly revealed by chlorosis. In the case of nitrogen-deficient chlorosis, the effects are first seen in the more mature leaves and tissues. The plant will preferentially export nitrogen to actively growing tissues, leaving the more mature parts of the plant to show signs of deficiency first. Nitrogen deficiency affects not only the leaves of the plant, but all living cells that have high nitrogen demands for amino and nucleic acids, reducing overall productivity and plant vigor. Generally, nitrogen-deficient plants also exhibit the spindly growth of an etiolated habit.

Phosphorus (P)

Phosphorus is frequently a limiting nutrient, particularly in tropical regions, where the soil chemistry differs from temperate soils, or in highly weathered soils, where phosphorus has long since leached away. Phosphorus is one of the three main elements in commercial lawn fertilizers, though there is mounting evidence that many lawns and green areas already have ample phosphorus, and thus it is being phased out of some commercial fertilizers.

The ultimate source of virtually all terrestrial phosphorus is from the weathering of minerals and soils in the Earth's crust.

Phosphorus is generally available as phosphate, an **anion** that is not bindable by the **cation exchange complex** (see Chapter 6) and thus can be easily leached from the soil by rain or runoff.

Phosphorus plays the same chemical and biochemical role in plants as it does in all other organisms. It is the main element involved in energy transfer for cellular metabolism and it is a structural component of **cell membranes**, nucleic acids, and other critical materials.

Plants lacking sufficient phosphorus are frequently characterized by phenomena that appear as wound-responses in leaves, such as production of pigmented compounds resulting in darkening or purpling of the leaves. Stunting can also occur, as well as necrotic lesions and other symptoms.

Potassium (K)

Potassium is the primary **osmolyte** and ion involved in plant cell membrane dynamics, including the regulation of **stomata** and the maintenance of **turgor** and osmotic equilibrium. It also plays important roles in the activation and regulation of **enzyme** activity. Potassium is a soil exchangeable **cation** and is actively absorbed by plant roots. It is a major component of many soils and is ultimately derived from the weathering of soil parent materials such as potassium-aluminum-silicates in the soil.

Potassium, though a part of the cation exchange complex, is only weakly held to the soil particles and is highly leachable. Due to plants and other organisms holding potassium as free ions in their cells, once an organism dies, its potassium quickly re-enters the **soil solution**. If other organisms do not quickly take up potassium, it is easily lost from the soil due to leaching and runoff. A loss of potassium is a common result of forest fires, clear-cut harvest methods, and other major disturbances that cause runoff and erosion.

Potassium-deficient plants generally form necrotic lesions or more generalized leaf necrosis after a relatively short period of chlorosis. In severely limiting conditions, there can be general bud death. As with nitrogen deficiency, symptoms of potassium deficiency first tend to appear in more mature leaves, as the plant will move potassium to actively growing, younger tissues. Most plants require potassium in fairly high concentration, and as a result, potassium is a common major constituent of commercial fertilizers, particularly in agricultural systems where the removal of plant parts (e.g., fruits) from the site strip potassium from the local cycling system. Sodium, another **monovalent cation**, can sometimes substitute for potassium in certain plants.

Sulfur (S)
Sulfur is another biologically ubiquitous element, playing critical structural roles in several amino acids and in compounds involved in electron transfers in photosynthesis and **respiration**. Sulfur is also a structural component of specialized enzymes and related molecules.

Sulfur is found in the soil primarily as sulfate and is derived from the weathering of parent soil materials or from byproducts of the human combustion of fossil fuels, which produce the sulfur-containing gases hydrogen sulfide and sulfur dioxide. These gases are converted to the sulfuric acid of acid rain.

Plants lacking sufficient sulfur often show symptoms such as chlorosis and spindly or stunted growth. Unlike plants deficient in nitrogen or potassium, sulfur-deficient plants generally first show signs of deficiency in the younger, developing tissues because sulfur is not easily translocated within the plant.

Calcium (Ca)
Calcium is a **divalent** cation that plays important roles in cell wall structure, cell membrane relations, and **signal transduction** in the plant. Most of these functions are essentially **extracellular**, occurring in the cell walls rather than within the cell membrane, though calcium's role in cell membrane integrity extends to the **intracellular** membranes as well.

Figure 2.2 This discolored leaf from a potato plant shows signs of magnesium deficiency.

Calcium is derived predominantly from geologic sources—from the weathering of soil materials—and is a major ion in the cation exchange complex of the soil. It is fairly uncommon for soils to be deficient in calcium, and most plants seem to grow under conditions with a surfeit of calcium.

In plants with insufficient calcium, developing buds, young leaves, and **root tips** either fail to grow or die, most likely due to cell wall related defects. Calcium is generally made unavailable to plants at low pH (higher acidity), so acidic soils often contribute additional symptoms to the calcium deficiency; many metals become mobile at low pH and are toxic (e.g., aluminum).

Magnesium (Mg)

Magnesium is another divalent cation but, unlike calcium, its roles are more intimately related to intracellular functions than the predominantly extracellular roles of calcium. Magnesium is the most import mineral in the activation of enzymes. Magnesium is also the central structural element of chlorophyll, and it is involved in the synthesis of nucleic acids.

The primary source of magnesium is the weathering of parent materials in soils and, like calcium, it is generally found as a common part of the cation exchange complex or in the soil solution. The solubility of magnesium decreases with increasing acidity and at high pH (alkaline) as well. In the case of low pH, magnesium deficiency will likely occur in conjunction with metal toxicity, due to the increased solubility of metals at low pH.

As magnesium plays such a critical role in so many aspects of plant cell biochemistry, there is no single pattern of symptoms for magnesium deficiency. Since magnesium is a necessary component of chlorophyll, plants that have insufficient magnesium often exhibit chlorosis (Figure 2.2). The symptoms of magnesium deficiency tend to appear first in more mature tissues because magnesium is translocatable within the plant.

Summary

Nitrogen, phosphorus, potassium, sulfur, calcium, and magnesium are the mineral nutrients required by most plants in the highest concentration, and thus they are defined as the macronutrients. Their distribution, function, original source, abundance in the soil, and physiological effects all differ, but their requirement for plant growth is long established. Because the requirement for these nutrients is quantitatively large, deficiency can be more common than for elements that are needed in only minute quantities.

Waste not the smallest thing created, for
grains of sand make mountains, and atoms infinity.
— E. Knight

SALLY'S HYPOTHESES AND FIRST OBSERVATIONS

After Sally set up her experimental treatments, she could barely contain her excitement. She checked on her seeds first thing each morning, when she got home from school, and in the evening before she went to bed. It didn't take long for things to start happening, and when they did, she was ready—making observations and taking photographs to use later in her science fair presentation. After the first day, she saw some indication that there were differences in the treatments. She reported her earliest results to her teacher with great enthusiasm.

He asked her about her hypotheses, and Sally tried to articulate them, but wasn't very clear. It was then that she realized that she should write what she intended to test in each treatment, what she thought she would find, and why. After writing her hypotheses and showing them to her teacher, Sally learned that in a more rigorous experiment she would have to make more detailed hypotheses, including the expected percent germination in each treatment and the rationale for her opinions in each case.

THE BASIC MICRONUTRIENTS

Micronutrients are the essential elements required by plants in relatively low concentrations. Micronutrients form a coherent group, including eight core elements: iron (Fe), sodium (Na), chlorine (Cl), boron (B), manganese (Mn), zinc (Zn), copper (Cu), and molybdenum (Mo).

Some scientists consider silicon (Si) a micronutrient. Though it not known to be essential, it is accumulated by plants and used in the plant body at a fairly high concentration. Cobalt (Co) is an essential micronutrient for plant species that form root **nodules** (see Chapter 9).

Additionally, nickel (Ni) is a micronutrient that, while essential, is virtually never limiting or deficient in the natural world. In the rare cases when it is limiting, symptoms include reduction in leaf size, cupping of the leaf, and reduced vegetative growth. It is also a component of a single enzyme, urease. When grown without nickel, plants fail to produce urease in sufficient quantity and can suffer effects of accumulating toxic quantities of urea in the cells.

Plants need micronutrients in low enough concentrations that the relative likelihood of deficiency is far less than for the macronutrients. Historically, our ability to identify the micronutrients has been limited by our ability to produce pure nutrient solutions without contamination. Some micronutrients are, in fact, common contaminants in other fertilizer products. Because the micronutrients are needed in such small amounts, even tiny proportions of micronutrient contamination in a nutrient essentiality experiment can skew or ruin the results.

Even in the field, micronutrient deficiency may be unlikely or known only in a few instances. However, for some micronutrients in certain parts of the world, the repetitive long-term crop harvest from a plot of land has stripped away these nutrients, resulting in soil conditions likely to cause deficiency (Figure 3.1). Symptoms associated with deficiency were gleaned from controlled laboratory studies in which micronutrient deficiencies were maintained by careful purification of all media involved in growing the plants.

For certain plant species, a given site may have insufficient quantities of a micronutrient and thus it shows a deficiency. If the same location were planted with a different crop with distinct nutritional demands, however, the amount and availability of the micronutrient could be sufficient for the new species. This differential need for mineral nutrients is a hallmark of plant nutrition research. Further, all micronutrients enter the soil solution by the weathering of parent soil materials. The rates of weathering and the availability of micronutrients are often a function of the pH (acidity or alkalinity) of the soil, and so soil chemistry and chemical changes caused by roots affect the overall availability of a micronutrient.

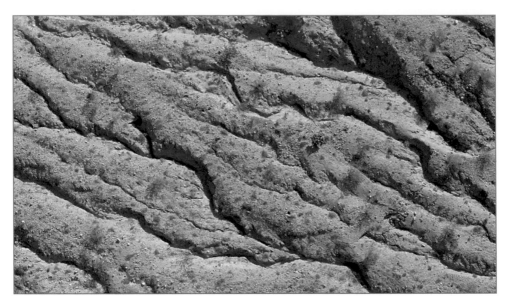

Figure 3.1 This dry soil has few nutrients left to spare for sustaining growth. Repetitive, long-term crop harvest from a plot of land can strip away micronutrients, resulting in depleted soil conditions.

Iron (Fe)

Iron is a divalent or trivalent heavy metal, depending on the **reduction-oxidation** conditions in the soil. It is intimately involved as a structural component of **heme-type** and other proteins, plays roles in the activation of some enzymes, and is involved in the synthesis of chlorophyll. Iron is found in the soil as various oxides and also in association with various organic molecules.

Iron can be limiting in the natural environment due to the unavailability to the plant of the oxide forms of the element. Plants overcome the limitations of iron absorption by either lowering the pH of the soil and thus increasing the iron solubility, or by the production of specialized iron-scavenging compounds called **siderophores**. Siderophores move into the soil, bind with the available iron, and are then reabosorbed by the plant. Once inside the plant, the siderophore is stripped of the iron and then sent back into the soil to secure more iron.

Plants deficient in iron show interveinal chlorosis, first appearing in the younger tissues because iron is not easily translocated within the plant body. In extreme deficiency, even the tissue around the veins becomes chlorotic, and the entire leaf may look pale yellow or white (Figure 3.2).

Sodium (Na)

Sodium is a micronutrient only for those plants that undergo **C4** or **CAM** photosynthesis rather than **C3** photosynthesis. C4 is

Detection of Plant Nutrients and Contaminants

Some scientific discoveries can only occur when other aspects of scientific knowledge have matured to allow careful experimentation. This is certainly the case with plant nutrition research. While the identification of macronutrients did not require sophisticated analytical chemical tools, the demonstration of the essentiality of the micronutrients was not simple a matter.

As micronutrients are required in comparatively tiny quantities relative to the macronutrients, they were often present in nutrient solutions as undetected contaminants. Thus, no matter how careful a researcher tried to be in determining the necessary elements for plant life, he could not determine the essentiality of some of the micronutrients, since they were unwittingly supplied to the plant. To discover these micronutrients, analytical chemical methods suitable to detect impurities and contaminants in the parts-per-million range were necessary. Lower detection limits allowed for a more precisely defined chemical content of the nutrient media, and facilitated the investigation of plant micronutrient requirements.

The fuller development of plant nutrition research was dependent on advances in chemistry, electronics, and industrial engineering to produce pure reagents for mixing plant nutrient solutions, and tools to confirm the purity of those chemicals. This is one brief demonstration of the interdependence of various scientific fields, and how advances in one area can encourage progress in another.

Figure 3.2 Iron deficiency can be seen in this hydrangea leaf.

a specialized form of photosynthesis that is more efficient in hot, dry weather. CAM is a specialized form of photosynthesis that greatly reduces transpirational water loss, typical of cacti and other desert plants. C3 is the most common type of photosynthesis, typical of plants such as maple trees and soybeans.

Sodium can also substitute for potassium to a variable degree, depending on the plant species (generally, species that are salt-tolerant can endure a greater rate of substitution). As a monovalent cation, it is a part of cation exchange complex and thus is available in the soil solution. The original source for some sodium is sea salt, but most of the sodium in the soil solution is from salts in the parent soil material.

Sodium deficiency is characterized by an inability to photosynthesize properly. In most soils and conditions in the field, a surfeit rather than a dearth of sodium is likely to be the case.

Sodium in high concentration in the soil can upset the **water potential** (see Chapter 6) of the soil solution compared to the roots and thus limit water flow into the plant.

Chlorine (Cl)

Chlorine is necessary for splitting water in photosynthesis, the step that generates oxygen gas breathed by animals. Chlorine is a monovalent anion found largely in soil derived from salts in the parent soil material. It is highly leachable, but is nonetheless available in large amounts, and thus chlorine deficiency is virtually unknown. In the laboratory, it is characterized by the formation of blue-green, shiny leaves that eventually turn a bronze color. In extreme cases, plants wilt or become severely stunted, in addition to having significant chlorosis and necrosis.

Boron (B)

Boron is a neutral micronutrient element, generally present in the soil solution as boric acid. The precise functions of boron in the plant are unknown. It is suggested to have a role in nucleic acid synthesis and general membrane function, as well as in cell wall structural integrity. Plants deficient in boron show general organ brittleness and the **apical meristems** often die. Roots can also die or become brittle. Such damage often leads to infection by pathogenic organisms, which have little trouble colonizing the already weakened plant.

Manganese (Mn)

Manganese is a heavy metal micronutrient, the functions of which area fairly known. It is involved in the oxygen-evolving step of photosynthesis and membrane function, as well as serving as an important activator of numerous enzymes in the cell, a role it can also share with magnesium in some cases.

The symptoms of manganese deficiency largely depend on the species of plant in which the deficiency occurs. In general, manganese-deficient plants form chlorotic and necrotic lesions on the leaves, fruits, or seeds. The distribution of symptoms, whether on younger or older tissues, is dependent on the plant in question.

Zinc (Zn)

Zinc is another heavy metal micronutrient that plays critical roles in many enzymes, often appearing either at the active site of the enzyme or in a position that regulates the enzyme structure. Lack of zinc results in the inability of the plant to make sufficient quantities of these proteins, and thus general growth and extension are limited. Zinc may also be involved in chlorophyll synthesis in some species, and in the synthesis of proteins from DNA.

The effects of zinc deficiency are both well known and dramatic. Specifically, plants deficient in zinc often show symptoms known as **little leaf** and/or **rosette** growth. In the case of little leaf, the leaves fail to expand to their normal, mature size. Rosette plants are those in which elongation of the stem is almost eliminated, so that all leaves appear to grow from the same place at the base of the stem. Zinc deficiency can also result in stunted growth forms.

Copper (Cu)

Copper is a micronutrient that is heavily involved in electron transfers in energy exchange reactions within the cell, due to its variable oxidation states. It is a component or activator of some enzymes. Copper is a heavy metal found in the soil in association with various other molecules. When found in the plant body, it is typically bound to special molecules within the plant to limit or prevent toxic effects that can arise from high concentrations. Plants deficient in copper often show symptoms of chlorosis or leaf rolling, though there is species-related variability. Woody species sometimes have bark that is blistered, and young **shoots** may experience dieback.

Molybdenum (Mo)

Molybdenum is a micronutrient specifically for plants that form root nodules with nitrogen-fixing bacteria, though plants that do not form nodules also use trace amounts of it in a protein involved with nitrogen metabolism and uptake. In the case of root nodule–forming species, however, molybdenum plays a structural role in the nitrogen-fixing enzyme nitrogenase.

The symptoms of molybdenum deficiency in plants that don't form root nodules include interveinal chlorosis, leaf rolling, and sometimes necrosis. In plants that do form root nodules, molybdenum deficiency results in a loss of productive nitrogen fixation, due to the bacterial need for the element (see Chapter 9).

Summary

Iron, sodium, chlorine, boron, manganese, zinc, copper, and molybdenum are essential for most plants. In each case, deficiency of the element results in significant, lasting damage to the plant or alteration of the way in which the plant develops. In many cases, the micronutrients (more so than the macronutrients) are involved as specific components of particular enzymes or proteins and so the effects of their deficiency are more subtle or specific. Any time a plant lacks sufficient nutrients, however, whether macronutrients or micronutrients, some physiological or morphological effect will take place, altering plant growth form, cellular function, or photosynthesis.

4 Plant Structure and Photosynthesis

Nature does not hurry, yet everything is accomplished.
— Lao Tzu

Plant Structure and Photosynthesis

SALLY MAKES MORE OBSERVATIONS

A few weeks have passed since Sally started her experiment, and she has learned some interesting things. In the treatments with both light and air, her plants have germinated and begun growing. Most of the plants in this group have developed leaves and are green and vigorous, but the plants are still young and she hasn't seen any major differences between the various watering treatments, except that the plants growing in the washed sand seem to be less vigorous than those in the soil treatments. When she noticed that these plants seemed to be wilted at the end of each day, she talked to her teacher about watering them more often. He told her not to do that, because if she changed the amount of water in one soil treatment without doing the same thing in other treatments, she would no longer have suitable controls for that variable; anything she might learn wouldn't be scientific information.

When Sally's teacher saw her dismay about this, he told her that all experiments have such disappointments—there is always something additional you could have tested, if you had known to test for it when designing the experiment. He reminded her that was why follow-up experiments are conducted.

Despite her mild consternation at this development, she was pleased with her experiment so far. Not a single seed in the no-water treatments had germinated, and none of the seeds in the no-air treatments had broken the soil surface. When her teacher suggested that she rinse away the soil in these treatments and examine the seeds, Sally was surprised. She was even more surprised at what she found: in all of the treatments that included water of any kind, but no air, the seeds had changed. Almost every one had put forth a **radicle**, though in each case it hadn't grown much. In her lab notebook, she noted this development. Her teacher asked her to speculate why the seed might be able to germinate without air.

It was at this point that she also examined her plants that received air but no light. In this case, the seeds had germinated and sent up tall, pale stems and little leaves, though by the time she examined them, they were dead and fallen. They had not greened, and there was little difference between the plants in the different water treatments. Soil type seemed to have some small effect on the plants, however, in that the seedlings growing in the sand were shorter than those in the two soil treatments. When she noticed that she now had data for most of the plants in her experiment, Sally told her teacher what she had learned so far and he asked her to write it down in her lab notebook and take photos.

THE PARTS OF A PLANT

To examine the limits imposed by the sessile existence that plants maintain, a few basic questions must be asked: What makes a plant? Why does it grow the way that it does? What does it require for survival? The answers to these key questions are essential for anyone interested in plant nutrition. Throughout the remainder of this book, the word *plant* will be used to speak specifically of the seed plants. Organisms such as ferns, mosses, and liverworts are indeed plants, but not seed plants, so they will not be considered.

The plant body is composed of two general domains: the shoot and the roots. The shoot is the **epigeous** (above-ground) portion of the plant, and the root is the **hypogeous** (below-ground) portion. The differences between shoot and root do not begin and end at their location, however. Over millions of years, plants have evolved specialized cellular organizations that differentiate organs from these domains in the plant. The differences in structure between shoot and roots have evolved specifically to deal with the important challenges posed by epigeous and hypogeous existence.

The shoot is divided into two component parts: the stem (including any branches) and the leaves. In most plants, flowers and fruits are also epigeous and thus can be considered part of the shoot. Stems serve three bas ic functions: mechanical support, conduction of fluids, and storage of biochemicals. Leaves are the main light-capturing organs and are the primary location for the bulk of photosynthesis carried out by the plant.

The Stem

The structure of a stem is dependent on the type of plant and that plant's life stage. For example, a seven-day-old seedling of a sugar maple tree (*Acer saccharum*) has a stem that is structurally similar to the stem of a bean seedling; both are nonwoody stems at this point in development. Examining those same stems four months later, one would find a very different structure in the sugar maple sapling. It would have formed a woody stem, whereas the bean stem would have remained nonwoody as it matured.

In nonwoody stems, the outermost layer of the stem, which is in contact with the external environment, is known as the **epidermis**. The epidermis is typically a wax-covered layer of cells that is impermeable to the movement of water. This impermeability helps the plant retain moisture and avoid desiccation. The layer interior to the epidermis is the **cortex**. Depending on the plant, the cortex serves different functions. In some plants, it is composed almost exclusively of thin-walled cells that serve in the storage of biochemicals. In many plants, however, the cortex often has strong, thick-walled cells that help to hold the stem erect, thus performing a mechanical function. In all nonwoody stems, the cortex is also the layer of cells in which the **vascular bundles** are embedded (Figure 4.1).

Vascular bundles are critically important structures when considering the plant body and plant nutrition, as it is through the cells in the vascular bundles that dissolved nutrients flow to reach the leaves and other organs. It is also through these bundles that sugar made during photosynthesis travels to organs that require it. The bundles have two domains, the **phloem** and the **xylem**. The phloem is the food-conducting tissue, and it

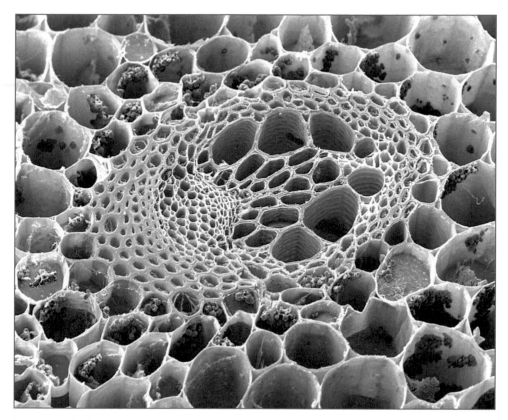

Figure 4.1 In all nonwoody stems, the cortex is the layer of cells in which the vascular bundles are embedded. This cross section of a buttercup stem shows an oval vascular bundle embedded in parenchyma cells (yellow-green) of the cortex. Some parenchyma cells contain chloroplasts (green). The vascular bundle contains large xylem vessels (center right) and phloem (orange).

conducts the dissolved sugars from the places where they are synthesized (typically the leaves) to the places where they are needed (the roots). The xylem is the water-conducting tissue, and it allows the flow of water and dissolved solutes from the roots continuously to the leaves.

Interior to the vascular bundles and the cortex is the central portion of the stem. In the case of broad-leaved plants such as beans, gardenias, sunflowers, and milkweeds, this central area of the stem is composed of small, soft, thin-walled cells known collectively as the **pith**. The pith is implicated in storage and synthesis of biochemicals, among other functions. In the case of the grasses and their relatives, the pith is absent, and instead vascular bundles can be found distributed throughout the stem.

Woody stems have rather a different structure. Woody stems are surrounded by the **outer bark**, which is a tissue that, like the epidermis, serves to protect them (Figure 4.2). Outer bark is a collection of dry, dead, and waxy cells that prevent moisture loss and can protect against other environmental woes as well (e.g., the thick bark of bur oak, *Quercus macrocarpa*, can insulate the interior living portion of the tree from damage from prairie fires). Interior to the outer bark is the **inner bark**. Inner bark is a type of phloem, and as such is responsible for conducting the sugar solution that is the food of the plant. Interior to the inner bark is a microscopically thin but critical layer called the **vascular cambium**, which produces the inner bark toward the outside of the stem and produces wood to the inside. Wood is the interior-most tissue of a woody stem and is responsible for conducting the water and dissolved nutrients from the roots up to the leaves. As it is a water-conducting tissue, it is considered xylem.

Leaves

The other main component of the shoot is the leaf. Leaves occur in many shapes and sizes, and this wide variety is a result of the many fascinating and elegant ways that leaves have adapted to the conditions to which they are subjected. With some notable exceptions (e.g., cacti, where the stems are the photosynthetic organs and the leaves have evolved into spines to prevent herbivory), leaves are the primary photosynthetic organs of the plant and as such have a form that is suitable to this function. They are broad and thin with a great surface area suitable for intercepting light and exchanging gases with the atmosphere.

The structure of a leaf is in some ways similar to that of the stem, but it has two epidermises, an upper and a lower epidermis.

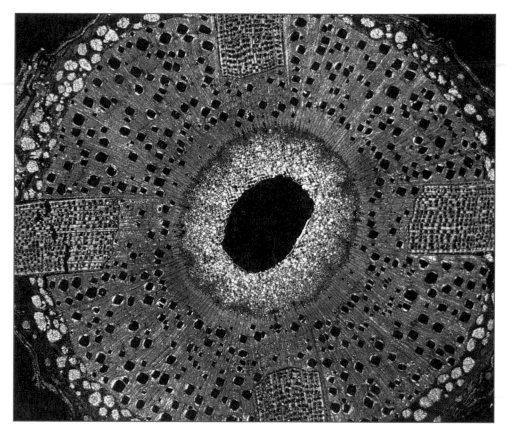

Figure 4.2 Woody stems are surrounded by the outer bark, which is a tissue that serves to protect them. Outer bark is a collection of dry, dead, and waxy cells that prevent moisture loss and can protect against other environmental factors. Interior to the outer bark is the inner bark. Inner bark is a type of phloem, and is responsible for conducting the sugar solution that is the food of the plant. This polarized light micrograph of a woody liana stem shows its dry, protective outer bark and its phloem-filled inner bark layers.

The upper epidermis is similar to the epidermis of the non-woody stem—it is covered with wax-like substances and serves to protect the leaf from desiccation and other environmental effects. The lower epidermis, however, is quite different. It, too, is typically wax-covered, but is perforated in many places by special structures called stomata, which are pores in the epidermis through which gas exchange takes place (Figure 4.3).

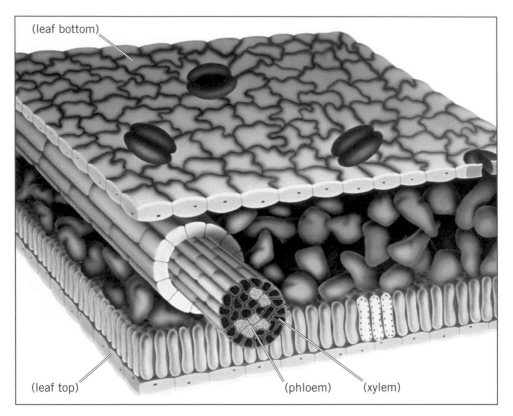

(leaf bottom)

(leaf top)   (phloem)   (xylem)

Figure 4.3 The anatomy and cell structure of a leaf includes the stomata (brown pores), spongy mesophyll (green), a palisade layer (yellow), a vascular bundle (center left), and a bundle sheath (orange). Within the sheath are xylem (pink) on the bottom side of the leaf, and phloem (white) cells on the top side.

Specialized epidermal cells that open or close in response to environmental and physiological conditions regulate stomata. This opening of the stomata is caused by the movement of potassium ions, often with chlorine ions as an electrical counter ion, into the specialized cells. The sudden influx of potassium causes water to flow into the cells, forcing them to swell and bulge, and the swelled condition of the cell opens the stoma due to a conformational change in the cell shape. To close the stomata, potassium and chlorine flood out of the special cells and water exits, allowing the cells to relax to a closed state.

Stomata on the plant body can be found on the lower leaf surface in most cases. An interesting exception can be seen in aquatic plants like water lilies (*Nymphaea* spp.), where the lower leaf surface is in contact with water and cannot serve for gas exchange. In this case, the stomata are almost exclusively on the upper surface of the leaf.

Between the epidermises of the leaf are the vascular bundles (known more commonly as leaf veins) and the **mesophyll**. The mesophyll of a generalized leaf is of two types, **palisade parenchyma** and **spongy mesophyll**. Palisade parenchyma cells are tall and columnar, found just beneath the upper epidermis of the leaf, and specialized for light capture and photosynthesis. Spongy mesophyll cells are oddly shaped, branching, and leave a significant air space within the leaf. These cells exist to help with gas exchange from the cells of the leaf to the outside air through the stomata.

Vascular bundles or veins are embedded in the various types of mesophyll. Leaf vascular bundles are structurally very similar to stem vascular bundles. The xylem and phloem of the leaf bundles serve the same functions as in the stem and are continuous with the stem all the way below ground into the roots.

Roots

Roots are the second main domain of the plant body, and are almost exclusively hypogeous. The function of roots is rather different from that of the shoot, and as a result, the structure differs accordingly. Roots are the primary water- and nutrient-absorptive organs of the plant body, and they also function in conduction of fluids, mechanical support, and biochemical storage for the plant. In the context of plant nutrition, the water- and nutrient-absorptive roles played by roots are the most critical (see Chapter 6).

Roots occur in various types, much as stems and branches do, and the type and function of a root may change over time within a given plant. All roots begin as nonwoody roots and thus share a common structure. The first root that emerges from a seed is called the radicle, and typifies this common structure. On the outer surface, the root has an epidermis. Unlike the epidermis of the epigeous portions of the plant, the epidermis of the root is not heavily covered with wax—wax would prevent the movement of water across the epidermis, which would be counterproductive to its function. Just beneath the epidermis is the cortex of the root. Unlike a stem, where many vascular bundles would be distributed throughout the cortex, the root cortex is a separate tissue. In the center of the root is the vascular tissue, which occurs as a vascular cylinder with alternating poles of xylem and phloem. The central location of the vascular system in the root is quite different from the peripheral distri-

Photorespiration

Rubisco (ribulose-1,5-bisphosphate carboxylase-oxygenase) is the enzyme that fixes atmospheric carbon dioxide to organic molecules. This enzyme is responsible for the fact that you and your loved ones are in the solid rather than gaseous state. When speaking of the carbon fixing function of rubisco, we are really only talking about one of the two enzymatic reactions catalyzed by this enzyme. Carbon fixation is the carboxylase function. The second function, the oxygenase function, is less desirable.

In an efficiently running chloroplast, there is sufficient carbon dioxide to be fixed readily by rubisco. In the natural world, however, carbon dioxide is in short supply, particularly when conditions are hot and dry. In those cases, the active site on rubisco will bind oxygen instead of carbon dioxide. When this happens, the oxygen is fixed onto an organic molecule (thus the oxygenase portion of the name) instead of the carbon dioxide. At first glance this might not sound like a problem, but it is quite costly for the plant.

The organic molecule to which the oxygen is fixed is now useless for making sugar without first detaching the oxygen and reforming the molecule,

bution of individual vascular bundles in the stem. Despite these differences in structure, the **vascular system**—root, stem, branch, and leaf—is functionally and topologically continuous. This continuity is maintained because, though the distribution of xylem and phloem differ in the organs, the actual component cells, their functions, and their interconnections are essentially the same.

This continuity of function across the plant body is indicative of the integrated nature of the plant as an individual. Each part and portion of the plant is built in such a way that permits it to function acceptably for the overall health and wellness of the plant and to allow it to capture sunlight and carbon dioxide to perform photosynthesis.

all of which costs energy. Thus, by fixing oxygen, not only is one "turn" with rubisco wasted, but also energy must be spent to reform the precursors of the reaction. Instead of gaining one carbon atom, the addition of the oxygen results in the loss of one carbon atom, due to complex biochemical processing. Oxygenation by rubisco results in the net loss of carbon dioxide, called photorespiration, as it occurs in the presence of light, but is independent of the energy-generating mechanisms of cellular respiration.

To minimize photorespiratory carbon and energy loss, some plants have evolved highly efficient alternate photosynthetic pathways that reduce or eliminate photorespiration. C4 and CAM photosynthetic pathways are ways by which some plant species have managed to circumvent the wasteful process of photorespiration, by simultaneously regulating the location of rubisco in the plant, and also concentrating the carbon dioxide accumulated by the plant in those rubisco-rich areas. This combination results in minimal photorespiration, and accounts for why C4 and CAM photosynthesis are more common in hotter, drier areas.

Photosynthesis

Photosynthesis is the production of reduced carbon compounds using water, carbon dioxide, light energy, and a variety of biochemical cofactors. It occurs in two main phases: the conversion of light energy to chemical energy and the fixation of carbon dioxide to carbon compounds using the fixed chemical energy taken from light. Photosynthesis takes in water and carbon dioxide, releases oxygen, and produces photosynthate.

Photosynthesis takes place in a specialized **organelle** within the palisade parenchyma cells of the leaves called the **chloroplast**. Chloroplasts are tiny green discs found in virtually all plant cells that are exposed directly to the light (Figure 4.1). It is in the chloroplast that many of the nutrients required by plants are concentrated. For example, a large amount of nitrogen, iron, and magnesium in the plant is found in the chloroplast, due to their roles as structural components of the enzymes and chemicals of the photosynthetic apparatus. Nitrogen and magnesium are critical components of chlorophyll, and without sufficient quantities of these nutrients, chlorophyll cannot be formed. Failure to form chlorophyll reduces the green color of the leaves, and thus chlorosis results. Iron plays a key role in many of the compounds of the energy-harvesting complex by which the light energy is converted into chemical energy.

Photosynthesis requires these nutrients to form biochemical machinery along with water and carbon dioxide to complete the cycle. The carbon dioxide used in photosynthesis comes from the atmosphere, and thus must flow into the interior of a leaf to be available to the chloroplasts for photosynthesis. To allow the influx through the leaves of carbon dioxide, an efflux of oxygen gas and water vapor from the leaf interior also takes place. This results in the net loss of large quantities of water. The evaporation of water from the leaf results in a **bulk flow** of water up from the roots to replace the lost water, and it is in this stream of water moving up the plant that most of the nutrients can be found.

Some types of plants, such as maize and cacti, have different photosynthetic pathways that help them deal with environmental conditions such as high temperatures (maize and C4 photosynthesis) or extreme water shortage and high temperature (cacti and CAM photosynthesis). Many aspects of these different pathways are similar or identical to "normal" (called C3) photosynthesis, but some aspects differ significantly and require additional nutrients not required to the same degree by C3 plants, such as the sodium requirement for C4 photosynthesis.

Summary

The structure and interrelationship of various organs of the plant are critically related to the ability of the plant to undergo photosynthesis, and will affect the distribution of nutrients within the plant. Structure alone, however, does not result in proper function of the plant, so in several cases, the roles played by specific mineral nutrients are for photosynthesis. Lack of mineral nutrients can result in numerous developmental and physiological ills for the plant.

5 The Effects of Nutrient Deprivation

Let us permit nature to have her way.
She understands her business better than we do.
— Michel de Montaigne

The Effects of Nutrient Deprivation

SALLY LEARNS THE DIFFERENCE
BETWEEN NECESSARY AND SUFFICIENT

When Sally showed her teacher her comments, he was pleased. He sent her to the library to look up the scientific meaning of two common words, *necessary* and *sufficient*. She learned that though these words seemed fairly simple, applying them to scientific problems requires precise reasoning. When she was getting a handle on these concepts, she used an analogy to have it make sense—that of a working, drivable car.

A car has many parts, systems, and features. Some parts and systems of a car are necessary for it to function; the wheels must be inflated and able to rotate, the front wheels must be able to be turned by the steering wheel, the engine must be able to take in and burn fuel, and so on. Each part is a necessary component of a functional car, but no single part is sufficient to make the car drivable.

Cars have other features as well, such as air bags, headlights, and turn signals. None of these features are necessary to make the car drivable, though they are important safety features for most people. Such features are neither necessary nor sufficient for the drivability of the car. Other features are necessary for the long-term operation of the car. For example, the radiator and cooling system of a car is necessary if it is to operate for more than a few minutes. So, necessary and sufficient can also have a time-component. There is no single feature in a car, whether short term or long term, that is sufficient to make it drivable. It has too many different interrelated systems, all of which have to be functional, all of which are necessary, for it to operate.

Sally returned to her teacher with a good understanding of necessary and sufficient. Air, water, and light are all necessary for plant growth, but none are sufficient. All three are necessary, and allow some plant growth, but not in the long term, because even together they are not sufficient. She was beginning to see that there were quite distinct differences in her treatments now.

SINGLE-PLANT RESPONSES TO DEFICIENCY

The effects of nutrient deprivation can be quite dramatic. General lack of vigor in a single plant is associated with several problems: reduced competitive ability of the individual, reduced **fecundity**, increased pest and pathogen susceptibility, and for crop plants, reduced **yield** per plant. These problems are not separate, and one may easily beget another as plant health declines.

A plant that is stressed due to a lack of nutrients cannot grow as quickly and lushly as its neighbor, and thus is likely to lose the race to occupy light gaps. This is often seen in mature forest stands. Small saplings will dwell in the shade of their parent plants for years and years, barely growing, biding their time. Then, one of the large canopy trees will fall due to age, lightning, or disease, and the space of the canopy formerly occupied by that tree's **crown** is available for all pursuers. The sapling that can most quickly reach that canopy position will have won the race for sunlight, and only a sapling well fortified with nutrients will be able to compete successfully.

An even more intense example may occur each spring in farm fields. In the case of maize, for example, farmers plant the corn when the soil temperatures are at an appropriate level. All the corn is genetically similar if not identical, and thus entire fields will germinate, grow their first leaves, and reach for the sun at the same time. If the farmer has followed the instructions of the seed company, the seeds will be planted in rows a suitable distance apart, with specific spacing between seeds so that each plant has the ideal and maximum amount of soil and space (Figure 5.1). This results in a well-ordered plot of land with each individual plant situated to grow to its fullest extent and produce its maximum yield.

Figure 5.1 Farmers plant corn when the soil temperatures are at an appropriate level. All the corn is genetically similar, and entire fields will germinate, grow their first leaves, and reach for the sun at the same time. The seeds will be planted in rows a suitable distance apart, with specific spacing between seeds so that each plant has the ideal and maximum amount of soil and space.

If, however, the farmer does not follow the guidelines and plants the seeds too close to each other, what could have been a productive field of maize growing with minimal competition between individuals becomes a silent gladiatorial contest, with each plant striving to outgrow its neighbors, colonize more soil, shade out those plants that cannot grow high as quickly, and hoard the limited resources of the field. These crowded conditions can reduce airflow between the rows, causing excess humidity that encourages pathogens and reduces the efficiency of gas exchange between the leaves and the environment.

For the plants in this field, some percentage of individuals (those that were able to secure larger portions of the resources) will produce yields approximately as high as each plant for the properly managed field, but many of the other plants, having secured fairly few resources, will never attain mature size or may die. The remaining plants that had some success and were not completely shaded by their neighbors may flower and produce an ear or two of corn, neither of which are full with fruits. Those kernels of corn are likely to be of lower nutritional value if used for feed and of reduced vigor or viability if used for seed. The total harvest from such an overplanted field will be far less than a correctly planted field.

FIELD-SCALE RESPONSES TO DEFICIENCY

In the maize field example, the underlying assumption is that the only concern is the plant's access to nutrients, light, and water. Ignoring light and water, what if the same farmer plants the field correctly, but the field is nutrient limiting and cannot provide sufficient mineral nutrients to the plants? Let's imagine that the farmer does not realize that his field cannot support a good crop of corn, and he fails to fertilize appropriately.

All of the nutrient deficiency symptoms for individual plants are also applicable at the whole-field level. However, there are also larger scale problems that arise from the same basic cause.

For example, if one maize plant is weakened due to lack of sufficient nutrients and is thus unable to defend itself against a pathogen attack, it may be colonized by the pathogen and even killed. For some diseases, such an outcome would mean the death of just one plant, but in many diseases, the sick plant will serve as a source of **inoculum** for its neighbors. Given that its neighbors are no better off physiologically, due to the general lack of nutrients in the field and the attendant lack of plant vigor, they will be as easily infected as the original plant. In such a way, a rapidly cycling disease can wipe out an entire

Statistics in Plant Science

How do you know when an observation is important? How do you prove it? Such questions are critical to modern biologists. In centuries past, biologists fit into two general types: experimentalists and natural historians. The experimentalists were those like J. B. Van Helmont that manipulated and controlled conditions and measured effects. Natural historians were those like Charles Darwin that made careful observations and interpreted the way nature behaves. Each type experienced problems—the experimentalists like Van Helmont often suffered from insufficient analytical methods, and the natural historians had no control over their subjects. In each case, the bias of the scientist could drastically affect the conclusions drawn by the observer.

In some ways, modern research is no different, in that researcher bias or poorly designed experiments can artificially alter the results of an experiment. There are still the basic questions. Are my observations important? Can I prove it? The methods used to answer these questions are statistical. Many people begin to shudder at the mention of statistics, but statistics are nothing more than another tool used to measure data, and like any tool, training and careful applications are required to produce good results.

field in a short period of time. If the entire field is producing the infectious units of the pathogen, it may serve as a source of inoculum to neighboring fields, and thus begin a plant disease epidemic (Figure 5.2).

A lack of sufficient nutrients for a given plant population or species can result in local **extirpation**. For example, if a logging crew cuts down all the trees in an area (a procedure known as clear-cutting) and then a replanting crew follows them to plant tree seedlings, the area will lose a large portion of the available nutrients in the soil to run-off and leaching. This is

Let's explore two basic types of statistics: descriptive statistics and hypothesis testing. Descriptive statistics are those with which you are may already be familiar, such as the mean, the median, and standard deviation. Most sports statistics are descriptive statistics; they summarize or encapsulate information in a specific way that makes the information easier to understand or visualize.

The second type of statistics is hypothesis testing methods. Hypothesis testing methods help a scientist answer the question, "What is the likelihood that the results I found are due to random chance?" You can imagine that if a researcher treats a group of plants with a new nutrient solution and half of the plants grow better than the other half, then the pattern could be due to random chance. If 95% of plants treated with a new nutrient solution show enhanced growth, then that might not be random chance. Hypothesis testing allows a scientist to assign an exact probability to the chance that 95% of the plants having better growth was random chance. Statistics have helped scientists determine the degree to which even subtle changes in conditions alter plant growth and productivity. A basic understanding of statistics is critical for aspiring scientists as it will help them design better experiments, better analyze their data, and make reasoned judgments based on their experimental data.

Figure 5.2 This corn field produced infectious units of a pathogen, served as a source of inoculum to neighboring fields, and resulted in a local disease outbreak.

because the clear-cut trees had helped to stabilize the soil and had served as biological repositories for the nutrients that cycled in the ecosystem.

The tree seedlings planted after the clear-cut will be growing on a site that is nutrient-poor relative to the original condition of the site. As those seedlings mature, they are likely to experience nutrient stress that will weaken them and make them more susceptible to other disturbances. They could, for example, fail to grow quickly enough to escape herbivory by deer or fail to out-compete noxious invasive species of plants, and that plot could lose the original tree species indefinitely.

Such a loss of a species can play out in three main manners: a temporary loss of the species and a delay while natural **succession** at the site progresses and the species re-establishes at that site, extirpation of the species at the site with replacement by other native species or invasive species, or a loss of that species and no subsequent gain of another.

ADAPTATIONS FOR NUTRIENT CAPTURE AND TOLERANT SPECIES

There are some plant species that are specifically adapted to growing in nutrient-poor conditions or conditions where the concentration of some particular element, generally a heavy metal, is toxic to other plants. For example, in the nitrogen-poor environment of a bog, there are carnivorous plants like the pitcher plants (*Darlingtonia* spp.) that form water- and enzyme-filled tubes into which insects fall or climb and cannot escape (Figure 5.3). Once trapped in the tube, the digestive enzymes of the plant break down the insect, and nitrogen and other nutrients are absorbed.

In South America, there are northern rivers (tributaries to the Amazon) that flood their banks each year and have done so for millions of years. Due to this regular flooding and leaching of the soil, there is little left but sand, resulting in a nutritionally impoverished site for plant growth. Many of the species that grow in this environment can be found nowhere else in the world, so they are called endemic to these locations, specifically because they can tolerate the seasonal flooding

Figure 5.3 Pitcher plants are carnivorous plants that survive in the nitrogen-poor environment of a bog. They form water- and enzyme-filled tubes into which insects falls or climb and cannot escape. Once trapped in the tube, the digestive enzymes of the plant break down the insect, and nitrogen and other nutrients are absorbed.

and exceedingly low nutrient content of the soils that other species cannot abide.

Summary

The effects of nutrient deprivation range from the decline of one plant to a diseased crop to the extinction of a species. Competitive ability and reproduction is decreased, while susceptibility to pest and pathogen infestation is increased. Light, water, and air must be monitored in conjunction with competition and growth patterns to reduce the risk of nutrient deprivation. However, there are some plant species that are adapted to growing in nutrient-poor conditions. These plants can grow in almost toxic areas and survive despite the low nutrient content of the soil.

6 The Rhizosphere

Nature cannot be tricked or cheated.
She will give up to you the object of your struggles
only after you have paid her price.

— Napoleon Hill

The Rhizosphere

SALLY'S LAST OBSERVATIONS OF OVERALL GROWTH

Sally was excited to record the last growth data for her plants, not because she wanted to finish the experiment, but rather because she wanted to have real numbers to show how everything worked out. She already knew from watching the plants for weeks that the soil treatments watered with nutrient solution had grown the best, but now she would be able to quantify it. She took pictures, made her observations, and recorded them in her laboratory notebook. Sally concluded that the plants grown in the washed sand treatment were small and unhealthy-looking compared to those in the soil treatments. The plants watered with nutrient solution were greener and healthier-looking, but also stunted and small, and made only a few flowers. The plants grown in the two soil treatments and watered with nutrient solution were healthy, green, and with flowers.

Sally was partly relieved to have finally made her last observations, but also she was a little disappointed. She had truly begun to enjoy the experimentation, observation, and informed reasoning involved in the project. Rather than kill her plants, she kept growing them, watering them with the same treatments she had used all along, and thought about what else she might learn from them.

WHAT IS THE RHIZOSPHERE?

Plant stems and leaves have fairly predictable lives: they live in air, which will vary in terms of temperature and relative humidity, but otherwise is essentially the same year round. Roots, on the other hand, live in an ever-changing world of soil, water, air space, and other organisms. This dynamic and complex environment is called the **rhizosphere**. It encouraged the evolution of a highly adaptable, efficient root structure that permitted plants to maintain their photosynthetic organs outside an aqueous medium.

Soil Water

Soil water is a critical component of the rhizosphere, as it is both the material in which mineral nutrients are dissolved and the source water consumed in photosynthesis and **transpiration**. Soil water occurs in two main forms, **bound water** and **free water**. Bound water is the sum of all the water molecules that are adsorbed by **hydrogen bonding** to the surfaces of the various soil components. This water, while important in governing some of the physical and chemical properties of the various components of the rhizosphere, is not biologically available to the plant or other organisms. Free water is the liquid water that fills the interstices between the various components of the rhizosphere. Depending on the overall moisture content of the soil, a continuum from no free water to completely saturated soils may exist. The amount of free water in a soil is related to the size of the soil particles; smaller particles can hold more free water than larger particles.

Air Spaces

All the spaces occupied by free water in a fully saturated soil could be occupied by air. Air spaces are critical because they allow oxygen for respiration to travel through the soil. Most **aerobic** organisms can tolerate only a limited time with no oxygen, and so fully saturated or flooded soils tend to encourage the growth of either **facultative** or **obligate anaerobic** organisms (organisms that can grow without oxygen, either as needed or requiring the absence of oxygen). Most plant roots have only a limited ability to survive without oxygen, so the air spaces of the rhizosphere, governed in part by soil particle size, is a critical aspect in plant growth and nutrition.

Soil Particles

The physical matter of soil is much more than dirt—it is a complex medium of many kinds of soil materials, each with different properties. It is the subject of entire fields of ongoing research. Soil is composed of two main classes of material: **inorganic soil materials** and **organic soil materials.**

Inorganic Soil Materials

The inorganic materials of soil are the minerals and compounds derived from the Earth's crust. These particles are largely composed of various types of oxides and silicates in conjunction with other elements and minerals. Most mineral nutrients of plants, with the main exception of nitrogen, are released from soil as part of natural physical processes. Soil particles range in size from roughly 2 mm (millimeters) in diameter all the way down to 2 μm (micrometers) or smaller. (A millimeter equals 0.039 inch; a micrometer equals 0.000039 inch.) A convenient scheme for organizing this range into size classes is as follows:

- Coarse sand particles have diameters from roughly 2 mm to 200 μm

- Fine sand particles range from 200 μm to 20 μm in diameter

- Silt particles range from 20 μm to 2 μm

- Clay particles range from roughly 5 μm to 0.01 μm in diameter

Note that this system has some overlap between categories. It is a necessarily artificial way of compartmentalizing the variation that exists (Figure 6.1). Each class of particles has associated physical and chemical properties that greatly affect their role in the rhizosphere.

The **water swelling capacity** and the cation exchange capacity are related to the surface area to volume ratio of the particle, which is inversely related to particle diameter. That is, large particles have less surface area for the volume that they occupy, whereas smaller particles have a greater surface area per unit volume. Clay soils, which have the smallest particles, have a high

Identification of Soil Microorganisms

When soil scientists or microbiologists study the microorganisms that live in the soil, they generally take a soil sample and then, after various means of washing and preparing it, smear the sample on a petri plate with growth medium at the bottom. They then store the petri plates at constant temperature and humidity, and after a few hours or days inspect the plates to determine what they have cultured. Such methods are time-honored, and are excellent ways of isolating and growing saprotrophic fungi and bacteria from such samples.

In some cases, the organisms in the soil are not saprotrophs. Some microorganisms are associated with other living things and cannot live or grow without them. Such organisms will not grow on a petri plate culture. In this instance, petri plate cultures should not be the only means of determining the soil fauna because they would misrepresent the number of species present.

With the advent of molecular genetic identification of organisms, it is possible to take a soil sample plate and extract the DNA from all the organisms present. Using additional molecular techniques, organisms present at the time of extraction can be identified by their DNA, and so even obligate biotrophs can be represented. Scientists have found that there are anywhere from ten to hundreds of times more species found by molecular genetic identification than by the classic method of petri plate culture.

This means that the soil, and by extension the rhizosphere, is biologically more complicated than was previously understood. As our knowledge of molecular identification grows, people will be increasingly capable of determining the nature and quantity of different species in the soil. As the coming decades unfold, it is reasonable to expect that our knowledge of biological processes in the rhizosphere will increase dramatically, also increasing our ability to provide for the mineral needs of plants.

Figure 6.1 A sample of soil in water shows the relative proportions by volume of sand (bottom), silt (middle), and clay (top). This method is used to determine the profile or type of a soil. The largest and heaviest particles sink to the bottom and the smallest and lightest remain on top.

water swelling capacity, because each particle can adsorb a certain number of water molecules. In the absence of these water molecules, the clay particles can be closely packed, but water adsorbs to the surface of the particles and occupies space, forcing the particles apart, and thus the soil swells. At the same time, the surfaces between soil particles are covered or filled with water. A sandy soil will experience little or no water swelling, as the slight absorption of water to the sand particles will not force the particles apart.

The second way in which particle size is important is in relation to the cation exchange capacity, which is the ability of soil to bind and release cations. Soil particles in temperate soils are electrically negative, thus they have an even distribution of negative charges on the surfaces of the particles, each of which provides a binding site for cations. In a soil with large particles, such as a sandy soil, there are few negative charges per unit volume of soil, and thus the number of available sites for cations to bind is reduced. In a clay soil, the number of negative charges per unit volume of soil is high and such a soil can hold a large number of cations. The cations held on the surfaces of the soil particles are in a state of dynamic motion, binding and releasing as tiny changes in conditions warrant. Common mineral cations bound to soil particles include ammonium, calcium, magnesium, potassium, and protons (+ charged hydrogen ions). There are also many organic cations that can be found bound to soil particles.

Nitrate, sulfate, phosphate, and organic anions are found dissolved in the soil water. Because they are in the soil water and are repelled from the soil particles, an equal charge of cations must also be in the solution. In this way, the water of the soil is a solution of many mineral and organic ions. The ability of a soil particle to release a cation results from the concentration of cations in the soil solution to be replaced with a cation of an equal charge. For example, calcium is a divalent cation and would require two protons as exchange to be released into the soil solution. This process of replacement of one or more cations with an equal charge of different cations is how the name cation exchange complex is derived.

Organic Soil Materials

Organic components of the soil include pieces of dead organisms in a variety of shapes, sizes, and chemical properties. Most of the organic content of soil that is not rapidly degraded by microbes is plant cell wall material, particularly **lignin**. Organic matter in soil can improve the water retention capacity, change the cation exchange dynamics, and improve mechanical properties of the soil by preventing compaction. It generally reduces the bulk density of the soil and improves aeration properties. It also can act as a substrate to a variety of microbes that play important roles in the rhizosphere.

Non-plant Living Organisms

Biological components of the rhizosphere are highly diverse. They can be macroscopic, earth-moving organisms, such as earthworms and ants, or larger organisms like grubs or other insects. All organisms in the rhizosphere represent high concentrations of minerals compared to the soil solution. As they reproduce, move, and die, they represent an important component of the cycle of nutrients in the rhizosphere.

Along with the macroscopic biota of the rhizosphere is an array of microscopic life, including protists, **nematodes**, fungi, and bacteria. Protists and nematodes have limited roles in plant nutrition, though they can be root pathogens (Figure 6.2). Bacteria and fungi can be plant-pathogenic, but they also have other important functions.

Hundreds of fungal species can live in a small amount of soil. Fungi are heterotrophs, so they must seek a food source in the rhizosphere, and they do so by growing long, thin threads called **hyphae** that quest for a substrate. Some species are saprotrophs, organisms that live by digesting dead organic material. Others, however, are **symbionts**, species that live in intimate association with other living things. Of the symbionts, some are parasitic or pathogenic on plants, and steal carbon or infect the roots

Figure 6.2 Nematodes are small worms that are found in many plants, water, and soils. A nematode worm is generally 1-2 millimeters long and often parasitic.

and cause disease and death. Some are **mutualistic symbionts,** those that provide some useful function to their **host** organism (Figure 6.3). The principal mutualistic fungi are the **mycorrhizae.**

Figure 6.3 A lichen is not a single organism, but rather is a combination of two organisms—fungus and alga. Although some of the fungi and algae that make up the lichen can live independently, many lichens are made up of fungi that cannot survive without its algal partners. Here we see lichens growing on the bark of a tree.

Mycorrhizae involve intimate associations between fungi and plant roots, where the fungus receives its food as photosynthate from the plant, and the plant receives an increased surface area and affinity for nutrient absorption. Thus, both partners in the symbiosis derive a benefit under normal circumstances.

The number and diversity of bacteria in the soil can be many times that of fungi, and they play similar roles in the rhizosphere, with some serving as saprophytes and freeing up nutrients that were bound in dead organisms. Other bacteria act as plant parasites and pathogens than can cause disease or dysfunction. Some soil bacteria remove nitrogen from the soil by using it as an energy source. Certain mutualistic species known as nitrogen-fixing bacteria, can infect the roots of certain plants and form specialized structures called root nodules. These nodules house bacteria with the critical ability to break the triple bond of gaseous nitrogen and reduce it to biologically available forms that the plant takes up for its own nutrition. In exchange for this valuable service, the bacteria receive a secure structure in which to live and carbon in the form of photosynthate.

Summary

The rhizosphere is composed of discrete abiotic and biotic components that form the complex physical and biological context in which roots must ply their trade. Each main function of the plant root—water absorption, mechanical anchoring of the plant, and the uptake of mineral nutrients—are effected by the specific components of the rhizosphere. In particular, the availability of mineral nutrients in the soil and the ability of plant roots to take up those nutrients are altered by changing conditions of the rhizosphere, and play important roles in the distribution of those nutrients within the plant body.

7 Nutrient Uptake and Translocation

If one way be better than another,
that, you may be sure, is Nature's way.
— Aristotle

Nutrient Uptake and Translocation

SALLY'S BEANS SHOW SOME SYMPTOMS

When Sally showed her observations to her teacher again, he was pleased, but he had additional suggestions. Sally took some notes as her teacher explained translocation of nutrients within the plant body. She went to the library, got a book that covered more about the topic, and decided to go home and make guesses about the symptoms that she saw in her plants. She knew that careful observation would be critical, and she had learned from the book that without actual measurements of the nutrients in the plant, which she would not be able to do, most of what she observed would be guesswork, but she decided to do it anyway.

At this point in her experiment, she had only those plants that were given light, water, and air. She had the two different watering treatments, distilled water and nutrient solution, and she had the three soil treatments—washed sand, autoclaved soil, and normal soil. Her first observations were quite straight forward: The plants grown in the two soil treatments, watered with nutrient solution, appeared healthy with no symptoms of any kind. The plants grown in sand were spindly, with smaller, yellow leaves. The plants in sand and watered with distilled water had died. The plants watered with nutrient solution grown in sand were not evenly green. The flowers did not seem to have set seed, and looked withered. Sally hypothesized that her plants were suffering from a lack of nitrogen.

THE ROOT STRUCTURE

A root grows from its tip, and can be divided conceptually into three main zones. Separate from these zones is the root tip itself, which is composed of the **root apical meristem** (the growing point from which all cells of the root are derived) and the **root cap.** The root apical meristem is a delicate structure and must be protected from the many components of the rhizosphere through which the root pushes as it grows. This protection is afforded by the root cap, a shield-like agglomeration of cells that, as the name implies, fits like a helmet over the root tip. The cells of the root cap are constantly replenished by the root apical meristem as they are sloughed off by abrasion with the environment.

Just beneath the root apical meristem, opposite the root cap, is the **zone of cell division**. This is the area of the growing root where cells are being divided off the root apical meristem and organizing themselves into the three tissue systems: the epidermis, the cortex, and the vascular cylinder (See Chapter 4). In this region, the cells are much like small boxes stacked together in regular files.

The next zone of the root is the **zone of cell elongation**. In this zone, the box-like cells are growing and elongating and it is this elongation that pushes the root through the rhizosphere (Figure 7.1). There is a high degree of coordination between the various cells in this region and the root tip, allowing the root to respond **tropically** (with directional growth) to various stimuli, such as toward the direction of gravity (positive geotropism) or away from light (negative phototropism).

The third zone of the growing root is the **zone of cell maturation**, and it is in this region that the bulk of the mineral nutrients are absorbed (except in cases of mycorrhizae) because it is in this region that the epidermal cells form specialized outgrowths called **root hairs**. Root hairs are tube-like cell wall extensions that grow more or less perpendicular to the surface of the epidermis and reach out into the rhizosphere as far as several millimeters. The importance of root hairs is a function of their high surface area and small volume—they provide a tremendous absorptive area to the root at a low energetic cost. Root hairs are also involved in the formation of mycorrhizal associations and in nodulation with nitrogen-fixing bacteria (see Chapter 9).

Farther up the root from the zone of maturation, the incidence of root hairs decreases and the roots often form a less permeable coating on the epidermis. Such an area on a root is no longer

Figure 7.1 Roots of a Lawson's cypress tree show the different stages of root tissue development. The tip of each root is white and the grayish-white region is where cell enlargement occurs. The brown tissue has stopped elongating and the cells are maturing

involved in water and nutrient uptake, but is instead involved in the long distance transport of those materials to the epigeous portions of the plant.

WATER POTENTIAL

Plant nutrients are water-soluble ions that exist in the soil solution at low concentrations. This means that the water potential (the measurement of the **potential energy** of the water, expressed as pressure) of the soil solution is close to but lower than 1.0, which is the water potential of pure water. Water will always move from an area of higher water potential to an area of lower water potential. Water potential is affected by many parameters, including gravity, physical pressure, and **osmotic pressure.**

In the case of the soil solution relative to the root, however, it is primarily with the osmotic component that we are concerned. The solute concentration of the soil solution is lower than that of the root cells, so the water potential of the soil solution is higher than that of the root. The tendency, therefore, is for water to **diffuse** *from* the soil *into* the root. On the other hand, because the concentration of solutes (nutrients) in the root is higher than in the surrounding soil solution, one might expect these nutrients to diffuse out of the root. They don't, because the **selectively permeable** membranes delineating the cells of the root prevent the nutrient ions from leaking out. In fact, the root cells must expend energy to continue to take up nutrients against the concentration gradient.

BIOLOGICAL MEMBRANES AND PASSIVE AND ACTIVE TRANSPORT

All the living cells in a plant are bound by a cell membrane. This membrane is formed of a sheet of chemicals called **phospholipids,** which impart special properties to the membrane. Each face of the sheet is composed of the **hydrophilic** phosphate heads of the phospholipids, and it is this property of hydrophily that allows intimate association with aqueous external and internal environments of the cells. The interior of the sheet is a double-layer of the lipid tails of the molecule, making the interior of the membrane a highly **hydrophobic** region. Due to this organization, the cell membrane is a highly organized, dynamic structure through which small charged molecules like ions and water cannot pass without special assistance.

Such assistance does exist, however, in the form of special proteins that span the thickness of the membrane and allow only certain chemicals across the membrane. This process of discriminating among various molecules imparts the property of selective permeability to the membrane. The proteins responsible for this, called **transmembrane proteins**, are found in great concentration throughout the cell membrane and they come in myriad varieties. The transport of proteins occurs in three major classes: **channels, carriers,** and **pumps.**

Channels are ring-like or tube-like transmembrane proteins that can open and allow the free and extremely rapid passage of various chemicals, depending on the type of channel and its configuration. For example, there are water-specific channels called **aquaporins** that allow the passage of water according to the water potential inside and outside the cell membrane. There are also potassium channels, which exhibit fairly high specificity for that ion and permit few others to pass.

In the case of potassium, which has a positive charge, the flow of the ion is in response not only to the osmotic gradient, but also in response to the electrical gradient. These two gradients are often considered together and referred to as an **electrochemical gradient**. For example, the interior of a cell could have a high concentration of potassium ions compared to the external environment, and thus the osmotic gradient would predict the loss of potassium from the cell. If, however, that same cell also had a high concentration of negative ions, the electrical gradient could bring potassium passively *into* the cell, despite the osmotic component. Whether channels are for charged or uncharged molecules, they can only allow transport along the electrochemical gradient, and thus they are considered passive transporters. They cannot accumulate their target molecules against their electrochemical gradients.

Carriers are much like channels in that they function in passive transport through the membrane, but unlike channels—which are open pathways through which the molecules flow—carriers have specific shapes that bind to their substrate molecules with high affinity. Then, after binding the substrate, they undergo a conformational change that assists in transmitting the molecule to the other side of the membrane. The selectivity of such proteins is generally higher than that of the channels, but the rate of transport is generally much lower.

The last class of transmembrane transporters is the pumps. Pumps are proteins that have binding sites for high-energy molecules such as **ATP** (adenosinetriphosphate, the primary form of energy currency within a cell) and another site for the substrate molecule. When the ATP gives its energy to the pump (by transferring the high-energy third phosphate group), the pump undergoes a conformational change and the released energy forces the substrate molecule across the membrane, even against its electrochemical gradient. Such a process of accumulating a chemical contrary to its electrochemical gradient is called **active transport**, and it is by definition a phenomenon requiring energy. Pumps are a common feature of most energy-generating systems in cells; they are common and essential in both photosynthesis and respiration. It is by running a pump "backwards' that ATP is made from **ADP** and inorganic phosphate, by permitting a proton to cross the membrane and thus contributing its energy to forming a new molecule of ATP, storing that energy in the form of a chemical bond.

ROOT UPTAKE OF MINERAL NUTRIENTS

The nutrients needed by plants are found predominantly in the soil solution, so by tracking the route that water takes into the plant, we can follow mineral nutrients. The pathway taken by water is a winding one, crossing several domains with critical limiting steps along the way.

Maple Syrup: Sap, Sugar, and Solutes

A steaming stack of pancakes calls for two things: a pat of butter and a reasonable dose of maple syrup. Most people know where butter comes from, and even how it's made. What about maple syrup? Maple syrup is made by boiling the sap from the sugar maple tree until the resulting liquid is thick, golden brown, and delicious. This is, of course, an oversimplification. The process takes many steps, each of which is more complicated, biologically speaking, than it seems.

The first concern is to get the sap from within the tree. Maple sap is extracted by driving a tap into the xylem of the tree, and letting the sap drain into a collection container. Sap flow does not depend on the generation of positive pressures in the stem, nor is sap drawn to the tap by transpiration, as there are not yet any leaves transpiring. Maple sap flow depends on a combination of nighttime temperatures below freezing and daytime temperatures above freezing; the freeze-thaw cycle is necessary for good yields of sap.

A large quantity of maple sap is needed to produce maple syrup. The amount of sap needed is dependent mostly on its sugar content, so the quality of the sap is as important as the quantity. A rough estimate of the amount of sap needed is 20-100 times the amount of syrup you want to make, depending on the relative sugar content. Sugar content, though an important predictor of the amount of sap needed, is not the only determinant of syrup quality.

Other solutes give maple syrup its odor and flavor. If maple sap were only sugar, no amount of boiling the sap would result in syrup. Increasing concentration and chemical reactions involving solutes other than sugar, all altered during the boiling process, result in the formation of flavored compounds such as vanillin that give the syrup its distinctive taste. At the bottom of the boiling pot, a residue of precipitated minerals is generally found; these minerals are often the very nutrients that the plant took so much trouble to accumulate, and they don't end up in the syrup.

Though the overall structure of the root has already been presented in some detail, two critical domains remain to be identified: the **symplast** and the **apoplast**. The symplast is the sum of all the contents of the cell membranes, which are continuous from cell to cell through special connections. This means that the symplast exists entirely within the cells, on the inside of the cell membrane. For a mineral to be in the symplast, it must have crossed the cell membrane through a transport protein at some place in the plant. Conversely, the apoplast is the continuous total of all the cell walls and spaces between cells, exterior to the cell membrane. The apoplast is largely open to the environment, at least for fairly small molecules, and there is no selective transport or discrimination in the apoplast. The apoplast can be considered an extension into the root of the soil solution.

Water and mineral nutrients follow a route that includes both the symplast and the apoplast. For example, water and nutrients from the soil solution may be in close proximity to a root hair. The dissolved nutrients may be at a lower concentration in the soil solution than in the root hair, but the selective permeability of the cell membrane is preventing the departure of the root hair's nutrients. Active transporters on the surface of the root hair's cell membrane can bind and transport mineral nutrients into the cell against their electrochemical gradient, and then they move through the root symplastically.

The water of the soil solution may tend to move into the root hair because the water potential of the soil solution is higher than that of the contents of the root hair itself. This water would then be likely to follow a symplastic pathway toward the vascular cylinder of the root. Other water in the vicinity, however, may not cross the cell membrane, but may move along the apoplastic pathway and thus come to the center of the root. In the latter case, however, there is a barrier at the boundary to the vascular cylinder of the root known as the **Casparian strip.**

The Casparian strip is a modification of the cell walls completely encircling the vascular cylinder of the root that prevents all apoplastic flow. It forces the water and solutes of the apoplast to make the transition from the apoplastic to the symplastic pathway prior to entering the transpiration stream of the plant. In this way, a root can discriminate against many deleterious materials and only allow across the cell membrane those things for which it has transporters and wants in the plant body. The Casparian strip is thus a last checkpoint for water and nutrients that have not yet passed into the symplast, a last way to take full advantage of the selectively permeable cell membranes and actively accumulate nutrients against their electrochemical gradients.

The root now contains water and mineral nutrients, the latter actively accumulated in excess of the concentration of the soil solution, needed by the epigeous portions of the stem. These substances must now make the trek from underground up through the stem and out to the leaves. This involves the bulk flow of water through the xylem of the vascular system. The water moves, as always, in response to water potential.

WATER FLOW IN THE XYLEM

Water flow in plants begins not in the roots but in the leaves, as they provide the driving force of the process. Actively photosynthesizing leaves are always using water, in part as a reactant in photosynthesis, but also for its evaporative cooling properties to prevent the leaves from overheating. Water use is also a necessary side effect of keeping open stomata for gas exchange and the capture of carbon dioxide.

A healthy leaf has high water content, with the result that the water potential of the leaf is much higher than that of the air outside the leaf. For this reason, water will tend to move from the leaf into the atmosphere as water vapor. As water in the leaf transitions from liquid to vapor, it exerts a small force on its liquid neighbors, pulling them "up" as it makes the transition.

This small force is propagated within the water column to the next water molecule, and the next, all the way down to the roots. This small force is a negative pressure—a tug upward—which reduces the water potential of the water just inside the leaf. This means that the water potential of the water in the xylem is higher than that of the leaf, and the water tends to move in that direction. This scheme, presented in a highly simplified form, is sometimes referred to as the **cohesion** theory of sap ascent, because it relies on the cohesive forces between water molecules to propagate down to the roots.

The resulting "upward" bulk flow of water carries along with it any dissolved substances: plant hormones, mineral nutrients, dissolved gases, and so on. This process is not active transport—the water is not being moved against its water potential gradient. Rather, it is a passive physical process, mediated by living organs: leaves at the top end of the transpiration stream and roots at the bottom. Furthermore, it is not a highly discriminative process; the plant has little ability to route nutrients here or there, as the transpiration stream is governed by demand for water. It stands to reason, however, that the increased photosynthetic and metabolic activity of water-demanding, and thus highly active, leaves would necessitate an increased delivery of dissolved nutrients as well. Many such nutrients, if delivered in excess of the needs of a particular leaf, can be reapportioned in the plant by transport in the phloem.

WATER AND SOLUTE FLOW IN THE PHLOEM

A significant amount of water also moves "downward" in the plant via the phloem, the photosynthate-conducting tissue that lies adjacent to the xylem in the vascular tissue of the plant (Figure 7.2). Bulk flow in the phloem is through a process sometimes referred to as osmotically driven pressure flow, where movement in the phloem is from photosynthetically active areas of the plant, called **sources,** to parts of the plant that

Figure 7.2 The veins in this aspen leaf are viewed as a network. The vein network carries water in xylem tissue and dissolved sugars in phloem tissue throughout the leaf.

need photosynthate, called **sinks**. It functions by actively transporting photosynthate into the phloem at high concentrations, establishing a strong osmotic gradient and thus greatly lowering the water potential of the phloem. As the phloem is immediately adjacent to the xylem, there is a ready source of water at much higher potential and water flows into the phloem. As more water enters the phloem, pressure begins to build.

At the sink location, photosynthate is removed from the phloem, increasing the water potential of the phloem until it is high enough to re-enter the xylem and make the trip back up the plant. Removal of water at the sink end of the phloem reduces the pressure in the phloem, so the phloem solution flows in that direction. Along with water, dissolved sugar, and many other compounds, the plant will also redistribute those nutrients that can readily move in the phloem.

The phloem-mobile nutrients are potassium, nitrogen, magnesium, phosphorus, sulfur, and chlorine. Nutrients with limited phloem mobility include iron, manganese, zinc, copper, and molybdenum. Some nutrients are phloem-immobile, most notably calcium, but also silicon and boron. With this information in hand, it may be easier to understand the symptoms of some of the nutrient deficiencies. For example, nitrogen is a phloem-mobile nutrient, and the nitrogen deficiency symptom of chlorosis is first seen in mature leaves, which are photosynthate sources, because it is being redistributed to developing leaves that are, until they reach maturity, photosynthate sinks. Because phloem transport can be highly specific from source to sink, targeted redistribution like that of nitrogen is more easily achieved when compared to nutrient distribution via the xylem.

Summary

The uptake of mineral nutrients across the root and translocation of nutrients, water, and photosynthate within the plant are governed by physical parameters such as diffusion and water potential, as well as involving implicitly biological processes such as active transport. An understanding of the way that a plant by itself will secure water and nutrients is necessary to appreciate the important roles in plant nutrition played by other organisms in cooperation with plants.

Shall I not have intelligence with the earth?
Am I not partly leaves and vegetable mould myself?
— Henry David Thoreau

Mycorrhizae

SALLY COMMITS HERBICIDE

When Sally went to her teacher with new observations and questions about the unexpected vigor of the plants grown in normal soil with distilled water, he again sent her to the library. This time she had to look up a symbiotic association between fungi and plants called mycorrhizae. To look for mycorrhizae, she would have to dig up and kill her plants. She was loath to do this, because then her experiment really would be finished, but she did what she needed to do. She took her plants out into the yard and used a hose and a bucket of water to gently wash away all the soil from each of the plants. Sally even did what she could to examine the roots of the plants from the other treatments that had long since died. Since the soils had dried out when she stopped watering them, the roots were in pretty good shape.

Sally was disappointed when she looked for mycorrhizae, as there weren't any signs of them that she could see. She tried using a magnifying glass to look at the roots, and though she saw some interesting things that she had learned about in class, like root hairs, there was no sign of mycorrhizae. When she told her teacher this, he nodded and explained that even if they were there, they would require special chemicals, stains, and a microscope to see. They didn't have those things available in Sally's school, so they couldn't look any further. Sally was again frustrated that she hadn't known to design her experiment in a way that would test for the presence or effect of mycorrhizae, but her teacher reminded her that all experiments, even the very best, could not test everything.

Somewhat relieved by this response, Sally mentioned to her teacher that she had noticed some funny things on the roots of some of her plants. She was certain they weren't mycorrhizae, but she didn't know what they were. After yet another brief discussion, Sally was sent to the library, this time to look up a different kind of symbiotic association.

MYCORRHIZAE

Fungi play critical roles in the biology of soil. They serve as decay organisms, breaking down the dead bodies of other living things and liberating their nutrients for their own metabolism and also for the metabolism of other organisms. Though this role in nutrient cycling is important, there is another, larger role played by the fungi in the rhizosphere—that of symbiont.

The parasitic and pathogenic roles of fungi were mentioned in Chapter 6. Both parasitism and pathogenesis are forms of symbiosis, but they are deleterious to the plant. The third type mentioned was the mutualistic symbiosis of mycorrhizae. Mycorrhizae are close associations between plant roots and certain fungi that result in several benefits for both the plant and fungal symbiont (Figure 8.1). Mycorrhizae are not some rare biological curiosity—the formation of mycorrhizal associations is the rule in plant growth rather than the exception, and some scientists have suggested that mycorrhizae were a necessary association for plants to invade the land from the seas. With the exception of a few plant families such as Brassicaceae (the mustard family), Cyperaceae (the sedge family), and the Proteaceae (the lacewood family), the vast majority of all plants in the world regularly form some sort of mycorrhizal association.

Endomycorrhizae

Of the two major types of mycorrhizae, the **endomycorrhizae** are by far the most prevalent, occurring in roughly 80% of all higher plant species. Endomycorrhizae are characterized by their apparent lack of effect on the root morphology and their pattern of infiltration into the roots of the plant host (Figure 8.2). They grow both between and within cells, and once within a plant cell, form special structures called **vesicles** and **arbuscules**. Vesicles are like small bags or sacs sequestered within or between plant cells and are implicated in energy storage and possibly as propagules for the fungus. Arbuscules are small

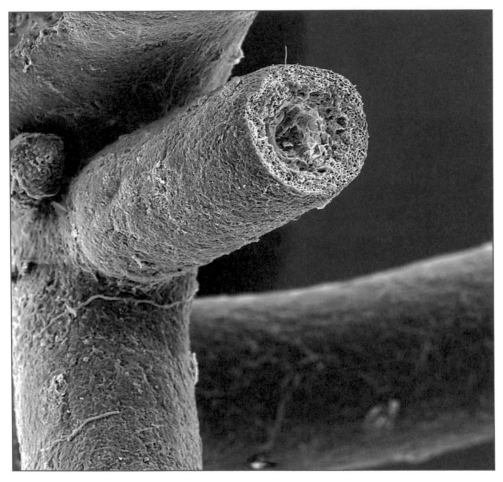

Figure 8.1 Mycorrhizae are close associations between plant roots and certain fungi that result in several benefits for both the plant and fungal symbiont.

tree-like collections of branched hyphae that occur within the plant cells. The thin branches of the arbuscule allow for a large amount of surface area to be packed into a single plant cell, and this relation between high surface area and low volume has implicated arbuscules in nutrient transfer between the fungus and the plant. Another name for the endomycorrhizae comes from these two structures, vesicles and arbuscules, the vesicular-arbuscular mycorrhizae (VAM).

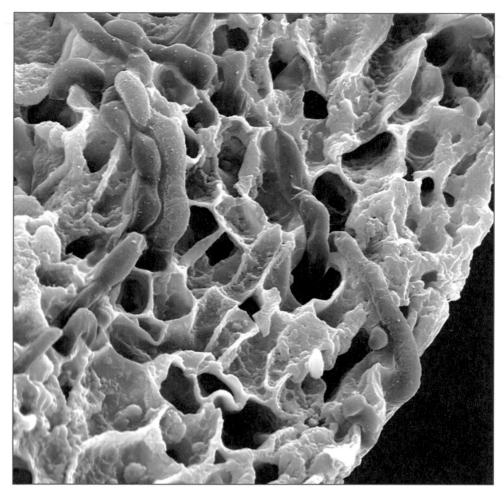

Figure 8.2 Endomycorrhizae are characterized by their lack of effect on the root morphology and their pattern of infiltration into the roots of the plant host. They grow both between and within cells (orange), and once within a plant cell, form special structures called vesicles and arbuscules.

Ectomycorrhizae

The second most common type of mycorrhizae are the **ectomycorrhizae**, so named because they form a thick sheath of fungal hyphae around the plant roots, making an obvious change in the morphology of the root. Ectomycorrhizae are typical of the woody species in the temperate portions of the world. It has been hypothesized that the thick mantle of fungal hyphae that envelops the roots of ectomycorrhizal plants imparts frost and freezing resistance to those species, by protecting the root to a certain degree.

Apart from the root morphological differences between VAM and ectomycorrhizae, there is also a major difference in the nature of the cellular integration between the fungus and the host. In the case of VAM, as mentioned above, the connections are both inter- and intracellular, with arbuscules penetrating inside root cells to form intimate associations. In the case of ectomycorrhizae, the fungal hyphae within the plant roots exist entirely intercellularly, and no hyphae enter plant cells. The degree of the intercellular penetration in ectomycorrhizae can be quite significant, however, resulting in a highly branched and articulated reticulum of hyphae, referred to as the **Hartig net**, named after the German botanist who first discovered it.

Ericaceous Mycorrhizae

The third type of mycorrhizae is specialized to the heather family, Ericaceae. In Ericaceous mycorrhizae, a notable difference is the relatively large proportion of fungus in the mycorrhiza— up to 80% of the mass in some cases. Ericaceous mycorrhizae seem to be specialized to handle the high-acidity conditions in which Ericaceae often grow. They are implicated in providing some resistance to the toxicity of heavy-metal accumulation typical in acid soils and also function specially in securing nitrogen for the plant.

Orchidaceous Mycorrhizae

The last type of mycorrhizae is specialized for associations with the Orchidaceae, the orchid family. In the case of some Orchidaceae mycorrhizae, the relationship between fungus and plant is not as clearly mutualistic as in other mycorrhizae. For example, some orchids make seeds so tiny that they have virtually no stored food of any kind for the plant embryo in the seed. When such seeds germinate, they are almost entirely dependent on finding the correct species of mycorrhizal fungus and then effectively parasitizing it until the seedling can become an established, photosynthetic organism. After that point, the utility of the fungus to the plant may be considered greatly lessened.

MYCORRHIZAL FUNCTION
The main effect of mycorrhizae on the host plant is the addition of significant surface area for absorption of water and nutrients. Associated with this increase in absorptive area is the ability of the fungi to grow into the rhizosphere at a much higher speed and lower energetic cost than the roots, and thus increase the total soil volume available to the plant from which to secure nutrients. Since the rhizosphere is spatially heterogeneous, such an ability to colonize and access a greater soil volume is an advantage over non-mycorrhizal species.

Mycorrhizae are most effective in securing phosphorus for their plant hosts. Phosphorus can be a limiting nutrient in many soils, particularly those that have a positive charge and thus strongly absorb phosphates. The fungal hyphae can strip the phosphates from the soil more readily than can the roots, and hyphae can extend beyond any locally depleted areas adjacent to the roots into unexplored soils. Mycorrhizae also help to absorb the essential micronutrients zinc, copper, and manganese.

There is also some evidence to suggest that mycorrhizae are less susceptible to root pathogens than plant roots without the symbiotic association. This appears to be particularly true for the prevention of root infection by pathogenic fungal species, which appear to be deterred by the presence of the mycorrhizae and cannot as easily gain ingress to the plant.

In nutrient-rich soils, plant species that would, under more limiting conditions, need to form mycorrhizae to flourish or survive reject the association with their symbionts, presumably to avoid the expensive photosynthate cost of maintaining the fungus. Such a facultative association with the symbiont implies that the plant may regard the fungal symbiont as an energetic parasite under certain conditions. Such a twist in the relations between symbionts is becoming more common as we understand in greater detail the intricacies of the associations between organisms.

Since plants form mycorrhizal associations most of the time, their importance in global plant nutrition and nutrient cycling can hardly be overstated. It is known that many species will only rarely complete their life cycles in the natural world if they are unable to secure a solid and lasting mycorrhizal association. Mycorrhizae play an integral role in the biosphere, helping plants achieve their goals of growth and reproduction. It is difficult to conceptualize this process at the global scale, but at smaller scales, such as a forest or the microcosm of a farmer's field, it can be more easily understood.

Most forest trees and other woody species in the temperate world incorporate ectomycorrhizae as a necessary part of their growth. It is thought that 90% of all such plants are mycorrhizal in the natural state. Mycorrhizae have been implicated in many forest health issues, including drought tolerance, resistance to insect outbreaks, carbon sharing between trees as canopy structure changes, and nutritional fulfillment of individual trees. The role of mycorrhizae in such a complex and unregulated natural environment is difficult to study due to the many interrelated and confounding variables, and so human knowledge of the role of mycorrhizae is growing somewhat slowly. Experimental forests and tree plantations, in which conditions are more carefully monitored and in some cases controlled, provide a simpler experimental system for studying these relations, but the long generation time of trees complicates our accumulation of knowledge on this topic. A place where we have been able to learn more, and faster, is in farm fields.

MYCORRHIZAE AND AGRICULTURE

Many North American farmers spend a lot of time and money applying chemical fertilizers to their fields to increase crop yield, and therein lies a dilemma. If a farmer fails to achieve good yields each year, he will lose money and possibly lose his farm. To achieve good yields, he spends money adding nutrients to the soil.

The Mycorrhizal Morel

Morels are wild mushrooms, prized for their flavor and texture by mycophagous epicures across their natural range. Morels are also a mycorrhizal species. This means that when you settle down to a dinner of morels, the carbon from which they are made was actually fixed by a tree and then "given" to the fungus in "payment" for services rendered. There is some evidence to suggest that as the fungus and the tree grow together, the morel has an excellent appraisal of the tree's physiological status. Thus, when the tree is stressed or dying, an abnormally large crop of morels may appear.

The morel is the fruiting body of the fungus. If it is not harvested by an eager animal (including humans!), its proper role is to produce and disseminate millions of spores, which act like tiny seeds or propagules to establish the fungus in a new place. The spores are blown away by the wind, and can carry significant distances to establish relationships with distant trees. In this context, the role of reproductive life raft is clearly relevant when the host tree is sick or dying; the fungus is signaled to "jump ship" and find a new and healthy host prior to the death of the current one.

The sudden appearance of many morels around a given tree is sometimes considered ecological foreshadowing about an impending loss of tree vigor, or as indicative of its decline. Due to the highly intertwined lives of the plant and the fungus in a mycorrhizal relationship, the physiological status of one partner is bound to affect the other. In the case of morels, the obvious and delicious result of those interactions may grow from the ground in the spring, providing a meal and perhaps also a hint about the condition of the host tree.

What might work better would be to carefully test and monitor his soils and the nutrient contents of plants as they are growing. If a farmer is armed with information about his soil and how the plants interact with it, he can better target his application of nutrients. By encouraging the plants to form mycorrhizal associations and thus secure less accessible nutrients from the field, he might possibly reduce the amount of fertilizer he applies each time.

We already know that plants with sufficient nutrients do not as readily allow mycorrhizal associations to take place. Thus, by fertilizing heavily, a farmer may be discouraging his crops from forming relationships with mycorrhizal fungi that would otherwise be formed if the plants weren't provided with a surfeit of nutrients. However, the only way to be sure that this plan will work is with careful monitoring and detailed experimentation.

Most major agricultural universities have special scientists whose job it is to consult with local farmers about how to optimize their yield and minimize the adverse financial and environmental impacts of their agricultural practices. Some state and local governments also employ such scientists, and they are generally called extension agents. Farmers can consult with an extension agent to discover alternative practices that may improve the financial and botanical health of their farm without having to carry out all the experiments themselves. Likewise, they might be able to provide some field space in which to conduct experiments in cooperation with a university or extension agent and thus gain scientific information about their farm that will help them determine new and successful methods of farming.

Summary

The variety of mycorrhizal forms and the specific ways in which they communicate with their hosts belie the similarity of function among the mycorrhizae. For the price of photosynthate from the plant (and shelter in some species) mycorrhizae colonize a far greater soil volume than the plant could cover for the same costs, increasing the available water and general access to nutrients. Mycorrhizae also can produce soil-altering chemicals that will change the soil chemistry and free up otherwise unavailable plant nutrients. They also play some role in protecting the plant from pathogenic soil microbes.

*Nothing is more beautiful than the
loveliness of the woods before sunrise.*
— George Washington Carver

Root Nodules, Nitrogen Fixation, and Endophytes

SALLY'S BEANS HAVE ROOT NODULES

Sally's readings assigned by her teacher had led her to the complicated world of root nodules and nitrogen-fixing bacteria. As soon as she saw the pictures in the books, she was certain that bacteria were on some of her plant roots. The idea of bacteria living inside her plants enchanted Sally. She read about the formation of root nodules and realized that, though she didn't understand all the advanced biology, root nodules were a specialized structure made jointly by the plant and the bacteria. Such an idea was not new to her—she had seen odd growths on corn and other plants in her father's fields and in their family garden caused by pathogenic microbes, but this was the first time she had actually seen a mutualistic symbiosis up close. With her newfound knowledge, she sat down and re-examined her plants, noting what she observed in her lab notebook.

There were many root nodules on the roots of the plants grown in normal soil and watered with distilled water. Sally thought that would explain why the plants growing in this combination of soil, water, light, and air were still mostly healthy even though they didn't receive a nutrient solution. The soil in the containers must have had enough of the other nutrients to allow the plants to grow, and the root nodules provided the nitrogen. She suspected that the reason these plants were a little smaller was either due to the energy spent making nodules and feeding the bacteria, or because it took some time to make enough nodules to supply the plant.

Sally sat back from her lab notebook with a sense of real satisfaction and began to prepare her final report and demonstrations for the science fair.

SYMBIOSIS AND NITROGEN FIXATION

In Chapter 6, we discussed the many roles of soil bacteria in the rhizosphere. Many species act as saprophytes, growing on decaying organic matter in the soil. Others are chemotrophs, harvesting energy from substances like nitrite, nitrate, or ammonium. Still others form special symbioses between bacteria and plants, and these symbiotic relations are the topic of this chapter. Such symbioses occur in the roots of certain species or families of plants and result in the formation of specialized structures on the roots called root nodules. Inside the nodules dwell the bacteria, protected from the environment by the plant tissue surrounding them. In exchange for this snug and reliable room-and-board arrangement, the bacteria provide the plant a valuable service: the reduction and fixation of atmospheric nitrogen to forms usable by the plant (Figure 9.1).

The fixation of atmospheric nitrogen is an energetically expensive proposition. Even with the correct enzymes, which plants lack, the formation of two ammonium ions requires the use of 16 ATP molecules, eight protons, and eight electrons. The enzyme that catalyzes this reaction is called nitrogenase and is actually an enzyme complex of six subunits that include the elements iron and molybdenum. Cobalt is also required as a part of a bacterial enzyme complex. Given that these elements play important structural roles in the proteins, they are critical nutrients for the nitrogen-fixing bacteria. When the plant forms an association with the bacterium, it necessarily takes on the nutritional requirements for the bacterium. In this way, root nodule–forming plants have different nutritional requirements than those plants that do not form such structures.

The most widespread incidence of root nodule formation is that between **legumes** and nitrogen-fixing bacteria of the broad general category known as **rhizobia** (Figure 9.2). The importance of this association is critical to human agriculture, because many of our crops, either as food for ourselves or as fodder for our livestock, are legumes: peanuts, bean crops, alfalfa, peas, clover, and many tree species. Apart from human agriculture, nitrogen-fixing legumes can also be important players in the ecological succession at sites with little soil, poor soil quality, or little nitrogen.

Figure 9.1 Nitrogen-fixing nodules on the roots of a pea plant allow the plant to utilize free nitrogen in the atmosphere and soil. Symbiotic bacteria living in the nodules provide the plant with the reduction and fixation of atmospheric nitrogen to useable forms.

When nitrogen-fixing species enter a site, they add nitrogen to their own bodies as they grow, but after they die, their nitrogen is available for local cycling among saprophytes and other plants that may be able to access some of that nutrient pool. As the number of plants at a site increases, the ability to cycle nutrients within the site increases, so if legumes are a persistent part of the flora of a site, the nitrogen content of the soil and of the biotic agents at the site in general can increase. Once the soil quality increases, less tolerant species can move into the site and continue to change the soils, tie up more nutrients in biomass, and increase the local cycling. In this way, plants with nitrogen-fixing bacteria can improve not only their own health, but also that of an entire site, by beginning the biological component of nutrient cycling.

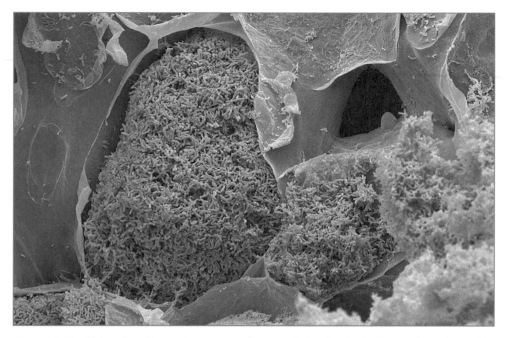

Figure 9.2 *Rhizobium leguminosarum* nitrogen-fixing bacteria (brown) are found in ruptured root nodule cells of a plant. Nitrogen-fixing legumes can be important in the ecological succession at sites with little soil, poor soil quality, or little nitrogen.

Growth, Care, and Feeding of a Root Nodule

While the overall import of root nodules and biological nitrogen fixation can be summarized in a few words, the real beauty and marvel of the process is not fully demonstrated without a foray into the molecular biology of the initiation and maintenance of root nodules. Unlike the case with mycorrhizae, wherein the fungus invades the root but the root does little in response to the entrance of the hyphae, the plant in cooperation with the bacterium actively forms root nodules. Prior to establishing symbiotic root nodules, the bacteria are free-living in the soil, unprotected, and the roots are of normal root structure. When the root of a nodule-forming species is growing, however, it produces chemicals that serve as attractants for the rhizobial bacteria. The bacteria travel along this chemical gradient to find the roots of a receptive species, and then prepare to make their entry through a root hair. If the entrance of the bacteria into the root were as simple as invading the root hair by force, the process would be little different from that of some pathogens. In the case of root nodule formation, however, the plant is a willing and active player.

Once the bacteria are adjacent to a root hair, chemical signals traveling between the bacteria and the root initiate the formation of a curve or a hook in the root hair. As the root hair curls around the bacteria, further signals stimulate the digestion of the root hair cell wall, and the bacteria migrate into their willing host, enveloped in an enfolding of the cell membrane called an **infection thread.**

Once inside that first cell, the chemical signals between the bacteria and the plant initiate the growth of the infection thread through the root until cortical cells suitably distanced from the epidermis are colonized, at which point the bacteria, surrounded in little sacs of plant cell membrane, migrate freely into the cells. Such membrane-coated bacteria are called bacteroids. The bacterioids stimulate cell division in the cortex, and the cells that divide as a result are the precursors to the root nodule. As the nodule develops and forms connections with the vascular tissue of the root, bacteroids make their way into the new cells of the nodule, and then begin their function, well sheltered from the rhizosphere and supplied with water and photosynthate.

At each step in this process, chemical signals traveling between the two organisms mediate the proper formation of a functional nodule. The structure of the nodule, while sufficient to protect the bacteria from predation by soil microorganisms, is not enough to provide the rhizobia with what they need to carry out biological nitrogen fixation. If the molecular biology of the formation of a root nodule is a marvel, the cooperation between the plant and the bacteria to optimize conditions for the chemistry of the process is also elegant.

Root Nodule Internal Chemistry

Root nodules must provide shelter, water, and sugar to the rhizobia as a part of the symbiosis. These things, while both necessary and significant, are not sufficient if the plant is to secure the benefit of fixed nitrogen. The root nodules must also provide an **anoxic** environment, because the enzyme complex nitrogenase is irreversibly inactivated by oxygen gas. To protect the enzymes of their symbionts, nodule-forming plants and their symbionts will cooperatively form a protein called **leghemoglobin**, an oxygen-scavenging protein that helps supply oxygen for bacterial respiration without affecting nitrogenase.

Leghemoglobin is an example of a specific compound produced solely in a root nodule—it is formed in part by the plant (the globin portion of the protein) and in part by the bacterium (the heme portion of the protein) specifically for the benefit of the bacterium. The evolutionary process that gives rise to a cooperative production of a protein like leghemoglobin is referred to as **coevolution**. Coevolution is the closely paired evolution of features in one organism in response to or in cooperation with another organism's changes or responses.

Coevolution of Host and Guest

In the case of root nodule formation, the coevolution of the entire process is tight enough that for most known plant-bacterium combinations, there are genes that code for signals to communicate between the host and that specific symbiont. Another species of either plant or bacterium would result in the failure to form a root nodule, even if the bacterium would be capable of symbiosis with a different species. Such specificity in colonization and nodulation is in contrast to many mycorrhizal associations, where the same fungus may be able to colonize dozens, if not hundreds, of unrelated plant species.

Agricultural Use of Symbiotic Nitrogen Fixation

Humans make good use of the formation of root nodules and the fixation of atmospheric nitrogen in several ways. The first and most obvious is growing legumes as food for humans or feed for animals. A second way is slightly subtler—the growth of **green manures**, where a crop such as alfalfa is planted and allowed to grow for a season and then plowed into the soil. This method is meant to introduce both organic material and nitrogen into the soil for the commercial crop planted the next season.

Another use for nitrogen-fixing legumes is **intercropping**, which is the planting of different crops in close proximity to benefit one or both species. Intercropping is particularly effective in small-scale agriculture such as a home garden, or in places of the world where most farming is done with human or

Industrial Nitrogen Fixation

The fixed nitrogen cycling in the biosphere comes from three main sources: atmospheric-fixed nitrogen, biologically-fixed nitrogen, and industrially-fixed nitrogen. Atmospheric nitrogen fixation is responsible for roughly 7% of the total nitrogen fixed each year. Of this atmospheric-fixed nitrogen, about 80% is fixed by lightning. During the extreme heat of a lightning strike, the triple-bond of gaseous nitrogen is broken, and nitrogen combines with oxygen and forms nitric acid, which is then deposited to the earth and the ocean when rain or snow falls. The remaining 20% of atmospheric-fixed nitrogen is fixed when nitrous oxide in the atmosphere reacts with ozone, forms nitric acid, and deposited it in the same way.

Biologically-fixed nitrogen accounts for roughly 63% of the total nitrogen fixed each year. The biological fixation of nitrogen is the largest input of nitrogen. The last source of fixed nitrogen is that fixed by human industrial processes. About 30% of all nitrogen fixed is accomplished in the Haber-Bosch process, where nitrogen gas is heated to several hundred degrees centigrade and put under enormous pressure in the presence of a

animal power rather than huge tractors. For example, farmers in South America will plant maize alongside beans, so that the nitrogen fixed by the beans can be in part utilized by the maize plants to produce both beans and corn in good proportion. For crops that are longer-lived, such as coffee, intercropping with a legume tree can provide enhanced nitrogen for the coffee bush and also shade to protect it from direct sun. Species in the genus *Albizzia* are often planted among the coffee shrubs in coffee plantations for these reasons.

Although not intercropping, the **field rotation** used by some North American industrialized farmers is a hybrid between the green manure approach and intercropping. By planting soybeans one year and maize the next, the nitrogen and organic matter left after the soybean harvest is added to the soil, contributing

metal catalyst. This energy intensive process produces ammonia to produce nitrogenous fertilizers. In fewer than 100 years, humans have taken an industrial process and scaled it to a point where the quantity of human-fixed nitrogen is more than quadruple that of atmospheric-fixed nitrogen, and is nearly half the biologically-fixed quantity. Almost one-third of the planet's yearly fixed nitrogen comes from human sources.

The Haber-Bosch process relies on sustaining high temperatures and pressures, the energy for which is derived from fossil fuels. Given that there is general agreement regarding the finite amount of fossil fuels in the world, it might be appropriate to wonder if humans can plan on sustaining that level of nitrogen fixation into the indefinite future. Without finding new, renewable energy sources to maintain temperature and pressure, it can be assumed that such production is not sustainable. Perhaps the way forward lies in understanding and exploiting the mechanism that already produces the lion's share of the world's fixed nitrogen–biological nitrogen fixation.

nutrients to the maize crop the next year. Once the maize is harvested and the soil is relatively nitrogen-depleted, another crop of soybeans begins the cycle anew the next year.

Non-Legume Symbiotic Nitrogen Fixation

Not only legumes form symbiotic associations with nitrogen-fixing bacteria; there are other plants and plant groups that have such associations, though they are with different bacteria. For example, alders (*Alnus* spp.) and *Casuarina* spp. form root nodules with another type of nitrogen-fixing bacteria from the genus *Frankia*. Plants associated with these bacteria form what are known as **actinorhizal** nodules, because *Frankia* belongs to a group of bacteria known as actinomycetes. Actinorhizal root nodules are less understood than legume root nodules, but the details of the symbiosis are similar: the plant provides photosynthate and shelter and receives fixed nitrogen.

In North America, alders are native plants, and the ecosystems in which alders grow are balanced. In the case of *Casuarina*, however, such a balance is not apparent. *Casuarina* is an exotic species in North America (not native to that part of the world). It is an aggressively growing tree and is becoming a problem species in parts of Florida and Hawaii. There can be little doubt that the ability of *Casuarina* to fix nitrogen in its root nodules plays some part in its competitive dominance over native flora, though such an ability is neither necessary nor sufficient to make an exotic species a noxious invasive plant.

Endophytes

Another type of symbiosis between nitrogen-fixing bacteria and plants occurs as well. This type of symbiosis is somewhat less complex than the case of root nodules, because the bacteria do not cause the host plant to form protective structures, but it can nonetheless play a significant role in the nutrition of such plants. Sugar cane (*Saccharum officinarum*) can receive nitrogen from nitrogen-fixing bacteria that live in its sugar-rich stem when nitrogen conditions of the soil are limiting. This type of association, where the bacteria live within the plant tissues in unspecialized association, is referred to as **endosymbiosis**. It is not limited to nitrogen-fixing bacteria, but also includes other bacteria and fungi.

Endosymbiotic bacteria and fungi are being regularly identified, particularly since the advent of practical molecular tools for microbe identification. In some cases, the role of the endosymbiont is unclear and may represent nothing more than a modest parasitism in which the plant shows little or no negative sign of infection. In other cases, however, endosymbionts can be shown to provide protection from or tolerance to stresses such as drought, temperature, or nutrient scarcity. Especially important is the production of compounds that deter herbivory or pathogenesis and thus protect the host plant from other organisms. As our knowledge of endosymbionts increases, we will have a progressively more refined understanding of the roles they play in normal plant growth and nutrition.

Summary

Root nodules are the plant-grown structures in which nitrogen-fixing symbiotic bacteria live, taking shelter and photosynthate from the plant, in return for removing gaseous nitrogen from the air and fixing it into biologically available forms which are then taken up by the plant. The association of a root and a nitrogen fixing bacterium is not haphazard, but rather relies on complex and intimately coevolved molecular interplay between host and bacterium to form the nodule, wherein the specialized nitrogen-fixing enzyme can operate. Nitrogen-fixing bacteria are not the only microbes living within plants without causing disease or injury; endophytic bacteria and fungi can also be found, and may play a role in disease and drought resistance.

10 Nutritional Quality and Global Change

In the end we will conserve only what we love;
we will love only what we understand; and
we will understand only what we have been taught.

— Baba Dioum

Nutritional Quality and Global Change

SALLY'S LOOKS TO THE FUTURE

Sally's science fair project was a resounding success. Not only did she get the highest grade in the class, but she also won the fair. Her project was going to compete at the statewide science fair at the end of the year. More importantly, though, she had learned that plants and plant nutrition were something she was truly interested in and also that she had a good mind for it. Her teacher called her in for a meeting again after the science fair and he suggested that she speak with the school guidance counselor about a career in science. The guidance counselor talked to her about college and graduate school, and Sally was thrilled with the prospect of doing more detailed experiments for her career.

The guidance counselor also convinced Sally to send the final report of her experiments to a professor at a local university who worked on plant nutrition. After several phone calls and a meeting with the professor and his graduate students, Sally got a summer job as a student helper in the laboratory. Although washing laboratory glassware was the main component of her job, she also participated in fieldwork to see experimental plots, collect field data, and process tissue samples for nutrient analysis. Sally was well on her way to a rewarding career in plant growth, plant nutrition, and **agronomy**, working to feed the world.

INDUSTRIALIZED AGRICULTURE

The previous chapters have focused on the biology of plants in the context of mineral nutrition, but perhaps the greatest importance of this information is the ways in which plant nutrition affects the human world. Plants are the world's water purifiers and air conditioners, the world's generators of oxygen, and most importantly, the world's food source. In what ways has the mineral nutrition of plants affected the food supply of the world?

Perhaps the most important historical and practical consideration is the industrialization of agriculture. With an increased understanding of plants' needs for nutrients and our ever-increasing ability to provide for those needs with chemical fertilizers distributed by mechanized farming operations, humans have been able to increase both the acreage suitable for growing food and the number of acres farmed per farmer (Figure 10.1). Rapid, reliable global transportation has made it possible to acquire just about any plant food at any time of the year from a major supermarket.

As we have come to rely more and more upon huge fields of genetically similar or identical plants growing at uniform rates, people have increasingly decried the quality of the food we eat. In many ways, this criticism is based on the intangible aspects of food production: flavor of products, the aesthetics of mono-culture, and other difficult-to-quantify aspects. One topic of concern, however, is the putative reduction in the nutritional value of the food itself. This is something that can be measured, tested, and recorded over time, and so should be easier to study. To examine this criticism, one must identify the idea of the nutritional quality of food and then further explore how modern agriculture and modern farming affects this quality.

Calories versus Nutrition

There is a critical difference between the caloric (energy) value and the nutritional value of food. In the developed world, the vast majority of people with dietary insufficiencies do not suffer from a lack of calories, but rather from an insufficient intake of vitamins and minerals. This is in contrast with the undeveloped or underdeveloped world, where there is an all too common lack of both sufficient calories and sufficient vitamins and minerals.

As an example, a person could easily take in all the calories they need for a day by eating sugar cubes or drinking vegetable oil, but they would lack virtually all the vitamins, minerals, and essential amino acids needed for health. Such a diet for even a few days could enfeeble a healthy person, and if it were continued indefinitely, permanent physiological harm or death could

Figure 10.1 Chemical fertilizers distributed by mechanized farming operations allow humans to increase both the acreage suitable for growing food and the number of acres farmed.

result. There is evidence for a decrease in the nutritional quality of modern food compared to what was available as few as 50 years ago. This line of reasoning is founded on two related trends: the processing of food including significant use of preservatives to maximize shelf life of products, and the generally reduced availability of homegrown produce. Foods are processed in many ways to ensure microbial safety by pasteurizing, boiling, cooking, canning, and the addition of preservatives, some or all of which are known to leach or break down some of the important vitamins present in plant foods.

On the second point, people often compare the flavor and freshness of remotely grown produce to what they can find in a local farmer's market or grow in their own garden, and find that the large-scale produce is inferior. There is certainly truth in this perception of reduced flavor in many cases, and the data seem to support that the nutritional quality of produce also decreases fairly quickly after being removed from the plant, unless it is processed immediately in some way that preserves freshness and does not damage fragile vitamins (such as freezing).

A "Perfect" Food Plant

We can now address a plant's ability to efficiently use the nutrients available to it, whether from chemical fertilizers, manure spread on the field, or what is naturally available in the soil and water (Figure 10.2). It is perhaps easiest to understand this topic by inventing a simple, hypothetical, "perfect" food plant.

A perfect crop plant would need minimal inputs of chemical fertilizers, would efficiently use the nutrients it has to produce a maximum amount of edible product, and that product would have a high nutritional value in terms of calories as well as vitamins and minerals. Such a plant would take up the nutrients it needs and no more, and after harvest it would leave behind organic material suitable for cycling the remaining nutrients back into the soil. The ideal plant would be economically desirable due to the low input of fertilizer and high yield. Notice that this ideal plant has stipulated the important parameter of nutrient content, not just total yield of product. This is a key way in which our hypothetical plant, and its hypothetical agronomy, differs from real-world production of food.

This critical difference is based on the developed world's dominant model of maximizing yield per unit area or unit time, with the minimum financial input in terms of time, machinery, fuel, fertilizers, and pesticides. The net result is a focus on the economic bottom line with little concern given to the quality of what is produced.

Consider this biological analogy: Aphids are insects that feed by sucking the sap from plants. Plant sap has an incredible quantity of sugar, which is the caloric basis of the aphid's diet. Sap has a very low concentration of other things needed by the

Figure 10.2 Plants are able to efficiently use available nutrients, whether from chemical fertilizers, manure spread on the field, or natural soil and water. Peanut crops are grown for food and for their oil. Peanuts are a type of legume that have bacteria in their roots that improve the soil by fixing atmospheric nitrogen to form essential plant nutrients.

aphid, however, such as nitrogen and other minerals. This has forced the aphid to evolve the ability to pass large quantities of sap through its body, taking up only some of the sugar that passes through it; most of the sugar is excreted. By processing huge volumes of sap, the aphid is able to secure the dilute nutrients it needs, but it wastes most of the sugar at a great cost to the host plant. This is almost akin to the expression "looking for a needle in a haystack" where the "haystack" is the abundance of sugar, and the "needle' is the collection of necessary nutrients.

Consider now the human equivalent: suppose one were required to eat nothing but potatoes, a food high in caloric value but with a relatively low concentration of vitamins and minerals, to secure complete nutrition. Ignoring some of the nutrients essential to humans that are absent in potatoes, a person might have to eat several times their necessary daily calories to secure a sufficient amount of nutrients that the potatoes. Unlike aphids, humans do not have the ability to pass most of those calories through undigested, so such a diet would result in massive obesity. Consider also the dreadful waste of those calories in a world where tens of millions of people suffer from insufficient caloric intake. For this reason, the world should focus as much energy on producing good yields of food with high nutritional value as well as economic value.

With regard to the nutritional value of food, the nutrient content of specific plant parts, those that we eat, are of critical importance. If the non-edible parts of a plant are filled with vitamins and minerals but the edible portions are bereft of those compounds, the food is of less nutritional value.

The ABC's of Yield Analysis

The main parameter a farmer uses for measuring the effectiveness of a particular fertilization regime for a crop, the nutrient use efficiency (**NUE**), is a combination of the nutrient utilization efficiency (**UTE**) and the nutrient uptake efficiency (**UPE**), none of which incorporate a concept of the nutritional quality of the crop. UTE is defined as the yield of the crop as a function of the nutrient absorbed by the plant, and UPE is the amount of nutrient taken up by the plant as a function of the amount of nutrient applied. The distinction between UTE and UPE is subtle, but important. UTE is at least somewhat dependent on UPE; if the UPE is low and the plant does not take up the nutrient, it cannot use the nutrient to increase its yield. Conversely, it can be the case that the UPE is high but the plant does not use the nutrient to increase the yield of the crop, thus UTE remains low.

Together, these two parameters give rise to the NUE: the yield of crop as a function of the nutrient applied. NUE is the easiest parameter to measure in systems where added chemical fertilizer is the main nutrient source for the plant, because farmers know the composition and amount of fertilizer applied and at the end of the season they have a precise measure of yield. UTE and UPE are more difficult to measure, requiring accurate chemical analyses of plant tissues during the growing season. The use of NUE, even when UTE and UPE are known, does not move modern agriculture any closer to monitoring and improving the nutrient content of the food produced, even if they are useful tools for agriculture as it is currently practiced.

Organic Farming

Organic farming relies almost entirely on natural sources for all farm inputs: fertilizers are manures (whether green or animal), pesticides are natural or not used, and manual labor frequently plays a larger role in the production of the food (Figure 10.3). Organic products are billed as being healthier, more nutritious, and better for the environment, due to the lack of major chemical fertilizer inputs. Organic products are almost invariably more expensive than those produced by traditional agriculture.

Critics of organic farming can be quite vocal, and their disputes with the organic movement range from economic to philosophical to scientific. From a scientific standpoint, two arguments in particular are of interest: the possibilities of severe microbial contamination of food that would normally be controlled by pesticide application, and the possibility that "unprotected" organic crops could host a major buildup of pests or inoculum that could move out against traditional agriculture. The former concern is perhaps the more severe of the two, because there are plant pathogens that produce potent toxins capable of killing or crippling a person in small doses. Realistically, however, if you practice basic sanitation, including washing any produce before eating or preparing it, you are unlikely to get sick from either organic produce or food produced by traditional agriculture. Perhaps the most cogent argument against organic agriculture is

Figure 10.3 Organic farming relies almost entirely on natural sources for all farm inputs, such as fertilizer made from manure, natural pesticides, and manual labor. Pictured here is a flourishing organic farm at the Center for Alternative Technology in Machynelleth, Wales.

its improbability of producing food in sufficient quantity to support the world's burgeoning population.

GLOBAL CHANGE AND PLANT NUTRITION
Despite the plaintive cries of some national policy makers, the effects of changing concentrations of greenhouse gases on the global climate are clear and present. Polar ice caps are beginning to melt, glaciers are retreating, and snow cover in some mountain ranges is decreasing at a rapid rate. This change in greenhouse gas content of the atmosphere, specifically of carbon dioxide, is of critical importance to plant biology and nutrition everywhere in the world.

With changing temperatures, the ranges of species will expand or contract. With changing precipitation patterns, flooding, soil leaching, and rainfall are expected to change. With changes in precipitation also come changes in plant ranges and in soil chemistry, which affects plant growth.

Just as important as the climate change, caused in large part by the increasing concentrations of carbon dioxide in the atmosphere, is the effect of carbon dioxide itself. In previous chapters, a brief introduction to photosynthesis was made in the context of the organic nutrition of plants, their accumulation and use of carbon, hydrogen, and oxygen. We learned that plants open the stomata in their leaves to allow gas exchange with the atmosphere in order to take up and fix carbon dioxide in photosynthesis. When those stomata are open, water vapor evaporates from the leaf, causing the upward flow of water and the delivery of the nutrients dissolved in that water (see Chapter 7). We learned, however, that the vast bulk of the water taken up by the roots is lost to the environment in this way, and that access to water is a critical concern for a plant.

When these facts are taken together, the idea of more carbon dioxide in the atmosphere might seem like a good thing. If there were more carbon dioxide per unit volume of air, the stomata could be less open, or open less often, and the plant could take up and fix the carbon it needs in less time, and thus prevent water loss. Perhaps the xylem water would have slightly higher nutrient concentrations and that would make up for less water volume. It is easy to speculate about the effects of such changes, but only real experimental data can truly help us make the correct choices over time.

Fortunately, there are experimental means to address these problems, and such experiments are underway and have been for some years. The United States has a system of research stations devoted to the study of ecological phenomena, including the effects of changes in carbon dioxide concentration, over the long term. They are called Long-Term Ecological Research (LTER) stations. Some LTER stations are studying the effects of increased carbon dioxide concentrations on plants in the field by constantly adding carbon dioxide to the open air in the vicinity of the study plants, but such experimentation is extremely expensive. A more common way to study this same issue is to grow plants in a greenhouse or growth chamber and control the carbon dioxide concentration and other variables directly.

Researchers have often found that plants do not react uniformly to increased carbon dioxide concentrations. Some plants grow more vigorously and use less water, as one might expect. Others grow more or less the same as they did without the carbon dioxide. Still others show reduced growth, and some even show symptoms typical of wound responses. Some plants try to grow more vigorously, but their nutrient requirements increase significantly, making them no longer profitable as crop species, because the NUE is much lower.

The best predictor of a plant's response to changing carbon dioxide conditions is the type of photosynthesis used by the plant: C3, C4, or CAM. In the case of C3 plants, it is hypothesized that increased carbon dioxide concentrations will favor such species. The increased temperature that goes along with increased carbon dioxide concentration, however, would favor C4 plants and to a lesser extent plants that use CAM photosynthesis, making long-term predictions difficult. It is clear that a topic as large and enduring as global climate change will have few clear answers, but rather will be the province of a new generation of scientists seeking to understand the effects of major human influences on the natural world.

Bioremediation

Bioremediation is the use of plants to clean up or detoxify sites. For example, on abandoned mine sites it is not uncommon for metal concentration in the surface soil to be one or more orders of magnitude higher than in normal soil. In such cases, many plants cannot grow on the sites that are left behind. Some species, however, not only grow and thrive on such sites, but they take up the contaminants into their own bodies, thus removing the pollution from the soil and making the site more amenable to colonization by other plant species. In some cases, this bio-accumulation is an accident, but in others people specifically plant the appropriate species in an effort to use bioremediation to cleanse the site.

Summary

The world is a rapidly changing place, in terms of politics, science, population pressures, and human disease epidemics. Famine is commonplace in some locations and unheard of in others. Access to clean water and nutritious food are the core issues forming the foundation of all economies, nations, and cultures.

If we were to assume that all land currently in agriculture would continue to be as productive as it currently is, with no loss of land devoted to agriculture, we could, from a purely nutritional standpoint, feed the world. These assumptions, however, are not sound. Ancient farmlands in places like the Middle East that have been irrigated for thousands of years are experiencing **salination** of the soil, resulting in the inability to grow suitable crops. The farmlands of North America are dependent on huge inputs of chemical fertilizers to sustain crop yields, and those fertilizers are manufactured using tremendous amounts of fossil fuel to provide the energy for the processes.

In what way does learning about plant nutrition help to prevent such a future? By understanding plant nutrition, we can identify future avenues of research that may help to alleviate some of these problems. For example, breeding or engineering plants that tolerate increased salinity may lessen salination. There are already such plants in nature, and by studying them we may learn to grow our crops successfully on such soils. By understanding the nature of nutrient uptake and efficient use within a plant, we might better target our application of fertilizers in North America. Furthermore, by understanding the soil and the nutritional requirements of our plants and our own bodies, we might produce plants to meet and not exceed those needs. By further understanding symbiotic relationships like mycorrhizae and root nodules, we could choose appropriate plant-microbe combinations and match those combinations to appropriate soils to produce the maximum yield with minimum input of chemicals, while still retaining profitability for farmers.

The options and possibilities for the future of plant nutrition are still limited more by human ingenuity, research, and technology than by the natural world. Armed with a sound understanding of our needs, we can target our energies to the most important problems and solve those first. Once scientists show that such efforts and endeavors literally bear fruit, people will adopt them and reap the benefits of an informed, sustainable agriculture.

Glossary

Abscission—The process by which a petiole detaches from a stem, resulting in the loss of the leaf.

Actinorhizal—The type of root nodules formed between some plants and bacteria from the genus *Frankia*.

Active transport—The movement of a molecule against its electrochemical gradient, requiring energy.

ADP (Adenosinediphosphate)—The lower-energy form of ATP, missing the third phosphate group.

Adsorption—The bonding of water molecules to tiny particles, generally by hydrogen bonding.

Aerobic respiration—The predominant type of cellular respiration that requires oxygen to generate energy.

Agronomy—The science of farming.

Amino acids—The basic building blocks of proteins; nitrogen-rich compounds central to life.

Anion—A negatively charged ion.

Anoxic—Without oxygen.

Apical meristem—The growing point or generative structure that produces the plant body found at the tips of stems and branches.

Apoplast—The sum of all the plant body external to the cell membranes.

Aquaporins—Transmembrane channel proteins that allow the free passage of water.

Arbuscules—Highly branched profusions of hyphae formed inside the cell membrane of endomycorrhizae.

ATP (Adenosinetriphosphate)—The main energy carrier used in cellular metabolism. Most energy transfers using ATP involve the transfer of a phosphate group to or from the molecule.

Autotroph—An organism that fixes its own carbon using an energy source.

Bacteria—Simple single-celled organisms..

Bound water—The water adsorbed onto small soil particles unavailable for plant roots.

Bulk flow—The mass movement of a liquid, generally water, in response to pressure.

C3—The most common type of photosynthesis, typical of plants such as maple trees and soybeans.

C4—A specialized form of photosynthesis that is more efficient in hot, dry weather; typical of maize (corn).

CAM—A specialized form of photosynthesis that greatly reduces transpirational water loss, typical of cacti and other desert plants.

Carriers—Transmembrane proteins specialized to permit only certain molecules across the membrane in the direction of their electrochemical gradient, generally in concert with the movement of some other molecule.

Casparian strip—A waxy layer coating the sidewalls of the cortical cells immediately adjacent to the vascular cylinder of the root.

Cation exchange complex—The distribution of negative charges on the surfaces of soil particles typical in the temperate world, allowing nutrient exchange and increasing the nutrient holding capacity of the soil.

Cation—A positively charged ion.

Cell membrane—The phospholipid bilayer that envelops the cell and delimits the internal contents of the cell from the external environment.

Channels—Transmembrane proteins that allow the free movement of a molecule across the membrane along its electrochemical gradient.

Chemoautotroph—An organism that derives the energy to fix its carbon from high-energy chemicals in the environment.

Chlorophyll—The green, nitrogen-containing pigment that acts as the main light-harvesting compound in photosynthesis, with magnesium playing a central role in the physical structure of the molecule.

Chloroplast—A subcompartment of photosynthetic cells composed of cell membrane and containing proteins, chlorophyll, and other pigments; the site of photosynthesis in plants.

Chlorosis—A symptom of nutrient deficiency characterized by a yellowing of the leaves, generally between the veins.

Coevolution—The paired or complementary evolution of features between two species that affect each other.

Glossary

Cohesion—The slight attractive forces between water molecules that allow them to transfer forces.

Cortex—In a stem, the cells that are not part of the vascular system, exterior to the pith and interior to the epidermis. In a root, the cells between the vascular cylinder and the epidermis.

Crown—The leafy top of a tree.

Diffusion—The motion of particles toward equilibrium as a function of random motion due to heat energy.

Divalent—An ion having a charge of either +2 or–2.

Ectomycorrhizae—A plant-fungal symbiosis in which the hyphae grow intercellularly, but not intracellularly.

Electrochemical gradients—The combination of chemical and electrical concentration gradients responsible for predicting the direction of chemical movements by diffusion.

Embryo—The young, undeveloped plant in a seed.

Endemic—Existing and native only to that location and nowhere else in the world.

Endomycorrhizae—A plant-fungal symbiosis in which the hyphae form highly intimate associations, vesicles and arbuscules, within the plant cells; also called VAM.

Endosymbiosis—A symbiotic association wherein bacteria or fungi live inside the plant without the formation of specialized structures.

Enzyme—A protein that exists to catalyze or facilitate a chemical reaction.

Epidermis—The outermost covering of the plant body in nonwoody plants

Epigeous—Above the ground.

Essential nutrients—Elements necessary for proper plant growth and reproduction.

Etiolated—Tall, spindly, pale growth typical of plants grown in the dark.

Extirpation—The local extinction or removal of a species from an area.

Extracellular—Outside the cell membrane.

Facultative anaerobe—An organism that can switch at need between aerobic and anaerobic respiration.

Fauna—All animal species in an area; used also to imply microbial life.

Fecundity—A measure of the number of offspring produced by an individual.

Field rotation—A method of agriculture in which two or more crops are grown in successive years on the same plot of land.

Fixation—The process of making an inorganic compound, such as gaseous nitrogen or carbon dioxide, biologically available by chemically converting it to a different form.

Free water—The water of the soil solution not adsorbed to soil particles.

Fungi—Essentially microscopic organisms that have long, thin, thread-like bodies; also includes yeasts, which are single-celled, round fungi.

Green manures—Plant crops that are grown with the intent of plowing them into the soil to improve fertility and other soil properties

Hartig net—The fine reticulum of fungal hyphae within an ectomycorrhizal root

Heme-type protein—A protein bound to a complex molecule with an iron atom in a central location, generally involved in energy transfer or transport of materials.

Heterotroph—An organism that secures both its metabolic energy and its fixed carbon by consuming other organisms, whether dead or alive.

Host—The individual in a symbiosis providing the food and or shelter; generally the larger organism.

Hydrogen bond—A type of weak and sometimes transient chemical bond; critical to many aspects of biology.

Hydrophilic—Able to interact or mix with water; salt or sugar are hydrophilic.

Hydrophobic—Unable to interact or mix with water; oil and wax are hydrophobic.

Hyphae—The thin, thread-like cells of fungi, with a high surface area to volume ratio.

Hypogeous—Below ground.

Glossary

Infection thread—The long, thin extension of cell membrane containing nitrogen-fixing bacteria traveling to the cortex of the root.

Inner bark—The conductively functional phloem of a woody stem.

Inoculum—The infectious material that causes disease.

Inorganic soil materials—Those parts of the soil that are not derived from living things, generally formed by the weathering of the Earth's crust.

Intercropping—The agricultural practice of planting complementary species in close proximity so that the properties of one species can benefit the other.

Internodal—The distance on a stem between nodes, which are the places where leaves or buds attach to the stem.

Intracellular—Within the bounds of the cell membrane.

Leaf—A thin, flattened organ of the plant specialized for gas exchange and light capture for photosynthesis; the main photosynthetic organ of the plant body.

Leghemoglobin—A protein produced jointly by the plant and nitrogen-fixing bacteria to mediate oxygen concentrations in a root nodule.

Legumes—A family of plants, Fabaceae, characterized by the formation of a pea-like or bean-like fruit; often associated with rhizobial root nodules.

Lignin—A plant cell wall compound that is highly resistant to most forms of biological degradation; provides the rigidity to the cell wall in tissues like wood.

Little leaf—A nutrient deficiency symptom in which the leaves fail to attain full size.

Macronutrients—Essential plant nutrients required in relatively large amounts in plant tissues.

Mesophyll—The parenchymatous tissue between the epidermises of a leaf that is not a part of the vascular bundles.

Microbes—Microscopic organisms, such as bacteria, fungi, protists, and some animals.

Micronutrients—Essential mineral nutrients required by plants in relatively small amounts.

Monovalent—An ion with a charge of +1 or−1.

Mutualistic symbiont—An association between two species in which each species derives some benefit and neither is harmed.

Mycorrhizae—A symbiotic association between a fungus and a plant root.

Necrosis—Dead or dying cells occurring in small patches.

Negative control—An experimental treatment intended to show that a facet of the experiment is necessary.

Nematodes—Microscopic roundworms that generally live in the soil; some are root pathogens.

Nodules—Specialized round structures found on the roots of some plant species when colonized by nitrogen-fixing bacteria.

Nucleic acids—Nitrogen-containing molecules that form the basis for DNA and other information-carrying macromolecules in the cell.

NUE (nutrient use efficiency)—The amount of crop yield per unit fertilizer added to the field.

Obligate anaerobe—An organism that can only respire in the absence of oxygen.

Organelle—A membrane-bound entity inside a cell, generally with a specialized function.

Organic—Chemicals that are generally produced by living organisms and containing the element carbon.

Organic soil content—The materials in soil derived from living things rather than from parent soil materials such as stones.

Osmolyte—Solutes responsible for determining the water potential of the solution.

Osmotic pressure—The force generated by water flowing across a selectively permeable membrane in response to water potential.

Outer bark—The dead, waxy protective coating on a woody stem.

Palisade parenchyma—The tall, thin cells just beneath the upper epidermis of a leaf specialized for light harvest and photosynthesis.

Parasitism—A form of symbiosis in which one symbiont harms the other and provides no apparent benefit.

Glossary

Parenchyma—A type of cell in the plant body, alive at functional maturity and responsible for virtually all biochemical reactions.

Pathogen—An organism that infects another organism, forms a lasting and close association, and causes disease.

Pest—An organism that eats or otherwise damages a plant but does not cause disease.

Phloem—The tissue of the vascular system responsible for conducting dissolved sugars from areas of production, such as leaves, to areas of use, such as roots.

Phospholipids—Molecules with hydrophilic heads and hydrophobic tails that form the basis of cell membranes.

Photoautotroph—An organism that uses light energy to fix carbon from the atmosphere to build its body.

Photosynthate—The fixed carbon produced by photosynthesis; generally a sugar such as glucose.

Photosynthesis—The process by which light, water, and carbon dioxide are converted into sugar, oxygen, and water.

Pith—The central-most soft tissue of a nonwoody stem.

Positive control—An experimental treatment intended to show that a variable causes change in the results.

Potential energy—The measure of the ability of a system to do work; a system with higher potential energy can do more work than one with less.

Protein—A complex molecule formed of amino acids; roles include enzymes, carriers, channels and pumps, and structural support.

Protists—Mostly single-celled, motile heterotrophic organisms.

Pumps—Transmembrane proteins that can move molecules against their electrochemical gradients by using the chemical energy of a molecule like ATP to actively transport the molecule.

Radicle—The first root produced by a seed as it germinates.

Reduction-oxidation—The addition or subtraction of electrons to an atom or molecule, changing its charge.

Respiration—The chemical process of extracting energy from sugar, used in some form by virtually all life on Earth.

Rhizobia—The general term for bacteria related to *Rhizobium* and involved in the formation of root nodules, generally with legumes.

Rhizosphere—The milieu of soil, water, air, flora, and fauna in which roots grow.

Root apical meristem—The growing point of the root from which all root tissues are derived.

Root cap—The shield-like or helmet-like protective layers of cells that guard the root apical meristem.

Root hair—The thin, cell wall outgrowth from a root epidermal cell in the vicinity of the zone of maturation in the root.

Root tip—The collection of root cap and root apical meristem from which all root tissues are derived.

Rosette—A plant structure wherein the internodes are short or nonexistent, resulting in the appearance of all leaves originating at the same place on the stem.

Salination—The accumulation in the soil of ions, generally sodium, that reduces the water potential of the soil and limits plant uptake of water.

Selectively permeable—The property of allowing only certain compounds across a cell membrane.

Sessile—Fixed in one location; unable to move; non-motile.

Shoots—The aerial portion of the plant body, composed of stems and leaves, that is responsible for energy capture.

Siderophore—A molecule produced by an organism to bind with iron, even at low concentrations, and then transports the iron back to the organism.

Signal transduction—The propagation of a molecular signal in one part of an organism to another part, generally involving an amplification of effect over time or distance.

Sink—A developing area of the plant where the photosynthate being consumed is greater than what is being produced locally.

Glossary

Soil solution—The mixture of water and dissolved mineral nutrients and other solutes in the rhizosphere.

Source—A photosynthetically active region in the plant that is making more photosynthate than it is consuming.

Spongy mesophyll—The oddly shaped parenchymatous cells just above the lower leaf epidermis, specialized for gas exchange.

Stem—The rigid portion of the shoot responsible for holding aloft the leaves and conducting sap and photosynthate.

Stomata—The openings in the lower epidermis of the leaf that permit efficient gas exchange with the environment.

Stunted growth—A symptom of nutrient deficiency wherein stems fail to elongate, leaves do not expand, and the plant is generally small and underdeveloped in appearance.

Succession—The natural progression of competition and life history in which the floristic composition of a site changes over time.

Symbionts—Species living in intimate association with other organisms such that at least one has a more successful life when in the association than out of it.

Symplast—The sum of all the interconnected intracellular compartments of the plant.

Symptom—An observable manifestation of a problem with an organism.

Transmembrane protein—A protein that spans from one side of the cell membrane to the other; generally involved in transport, signal transduction, or energy generation.

Transpiration—The process by which plant leaves lose water to the atmosphere, cooling them and providing the driving force for long-distance water movement in the plant.

Treatment—A set of experimental conditions to test a single variable.

Tropically—Growing directionally in response to a stimulus; positive tropisms are toward the stimulus, while negative tropisms are away from the stimulus.

Turgor—The pressure exerted on the cell wall by the cell membrane, keeping the herbaceous parts of the plant rigid.

UPE (nutrient uptake efficiency)—The amount of nutrient absorbed per unit nutrient applied.

UTE (nutrient utilization efficiency)—The crop yield per unit of nutrient absorbed.

Vascular bundles—The long, continuous associations of xylem elements and phloem elements into one structure; known as veins when seen in leaves.

Vascular cambium—The lateral meristem between the wood and the inner bark; responsible for the production of wood to the inside and inner bark to the outside.

Vascular system—The collection of all the vascular bundles and other vascular tissue throughout the plant.

Veins—The vascular bundles of leaves.

Vesicles—The balloon-like or spore-like structures formed inside plant cells by endomycorrhizal hyphae.

Water potential—The measurement of the potential energy of water in a given context; the predictor of water movement.

Water swelling capacity—The degree to which the adsorption of water onto the surfaces of soil particles affects the bulk volume of the soil particles.

Xylem—The water- or sap-conducting tissue of the vascular system.

Yield—The amount of crop harvested at the end of the growing season.

Zone of cell division—The region of the root just behind the root apical meristem where the cells actively divide.

Zone of cell elongation—The region of the root just behind the zone of cell division where the cells actively elongate and push the root through the soil.

Zone of cell maturation—The region of the root just behind the zone of cell elongation where root hairs begin to form; this area of the root is responsible for the bulk of the nutrient and water uptake in the plant.

Bibliography

Agrios, G. *Plant Pathology*, 3rd ed. San Diego, CA: Academic Press, 1988.

Anderson, S., A. Chappelka, K. Flynn, J. Odom. "Lead Accumulation in *Quercus nigra* and *Q. velutina* Near Smelting Facilities in Alabama, USA." *Water, Air and Soil Pollution* 118 (2000): 1–11.

Canny, M. "A New Theory for the Ascent of Sap-cohesion Supported by Tissue Pressure." *Annals of Botany* 75 (1995): 343–357.

Clarkson, D. "Factors Affecting Mineral Nutrient Acquisition by Plants." *Annual Review of Plant Physiology* 36 (1985): 77–115.

Clarkson, D., and J. Hanson. "The Mineral Nutrition of Higher Plants." *Annual Review of Plant Physiology* 31 (1980): 239–298.

Epstein, E., and A. Bloom. *Mineral Nutrition of Plants: Principles and Perspectives*, 2nd ed. Sunderland, MA: Sinauer Associates, 2005.

Esau, K. *Anatomy of Seed Plants*, 2nd ed. New York: John Wiley and Sons, 1977.

Hinsinger, P. "How Do Plant Roots Acquire Mineral Nutrients? Chemical Processes Involved in the Rhizosphere." *Advances in Agronomy* 64 (1998): 225–265.

Lam, K., G. Ottewill, B. Plunkett, F. Walsh. "Lead at the Roadside." *Green Chemistry* (1999): 105–109.

Lodish, H., A. Berk, L. Zipursky, P. Matsudaira, D. Baltimore, J. Darnell, *Molecular Cell Biology*, 4th ed. New York: W. H. Freeman, 2000.

McCully, M. "How Do Real Roots Work—Some New Views of Root Structure." *Plant Physiology* 109 (1995): 1–6.

Peterson, R., and M. Farquhar. "Root Hairs: Specialized Tubular Cells Extending Root Surfaces." *Botanical Review* 62 (1996): 1–40.

Raven, P., R. Evert, S. Eichhorn. *Biology of Plants*, 5th ed. New York: Worth, 1992.

Stitt, M., et al. "Step Towards an Integrated View of Nitrogen Metabolism." *Journal of Experimental Botany* 53 (2002): 959–970.

Stout, P., and R. Overstreet. "Soil Chemistry in Relation to Inorganic Nutrition of Plants." *Annual Review of Plant Physiology* 1 (1950): 305–342.

Taiz, L., and E. Zeiger. *Plant Physiology*. Redwood City, CA: Benjamin/Cummings, 1991.

Tyree, M. "The Cohesion-tension Theory of Sap Ascent—Current Controversies." *Journal of Experimental Botany* 48 (1997): 1753–1765.

Van der Ploeg, R., W. Bohm, M. Kirkham. "On the Origin of the Theory of Mineral Nutrition of Plants and the Law of the Minimum." *Soil Science Society of America Journal* 63 (1999): 1055–1062.

Welch, R. "Micronutrient Nutrition of Plants." *Critical Reviews in Plant Science* 14 (1995): 49–82.

Zwieniecki, M., P. Melcher, N. Holbrook. "Hydrogel Control of Xylem Hydraulic Resistance in Plants." *Science* 291 (2001): 1059–1062.

Further Reading

Bailey, Jill, ed. *The Facts on File Dictionary of Botany.* New York: Facts on File, 2002.

Capon, Brian. *Botany for Gardeners.* Portland, OR: Timber Press, 2005.

Dashefsky, Steven H. *Botany: High-School Science Fair Experiments.* Blue Ridge Summit, PA: TAB Books, 1995.

Epstein, E. and A. Bloom. *Mineral Nutrition of Plants: Principles and Perspectives.* Sunderland, MA: Sinauer Associates, 2005.

Jones, J. Benton, Jr. *Plant Nutrition Manual.* Boca Raton, FL: CRC Press, 1998.

Mengel, Konrad, and Ernest A. Kirkby. *Principles of Plant Nutrition.* Boston: Kluwer Academic Publishers, 2001.

Websites
Botanical Society of America
http://www.botany.org.

Botany Online—The Internet Hypertextbook
http://www.biologie.uni-hamburg.de/b-online/e00/contents.htm

National Biological Information Infrastructure
http://www.nbii.gov/disciplines/botany/

Smithsonian National Museum of Natural History
http://www.mnh.si.edu/

Index

Index

Saprophytes, 73, 102
Saprotrophs, 67, 70
Selective permeability, 79, 133
Shoots, 39, 133
Siderophores, 30, 133
Signal transduction, 23, 133
Silicon, 28, 87
Silt, 66, 68
Sinks, 86, 87, 133
Sodium, 23, 31-33
Soil materials, 65-66, 66-69, 70, 130, 131
Soil solutions, 22, 32, 134
Solutes, 85-87
Spongy mesophyll, 44, 45, 134
Statistics, 56-57
Stems, 40-42, 134
Stomata, 22, 43-45, 134
Succession, 59, 134
Sulfur, 6, 23, 87
Surface area, 95
Swelling capacity, 66-69, 135
Symbiosis, 70-71, 102-104, 134. *See also* Endosymbiosis; Mutualistic symbionts; Mycorrhizae
Symplast, 83-84, 134

Threads, infection, 106, 130
Transmembrane proteins, 80, 134
Transpiration, 65, 134
Transport, 79-81
Tropisms, 77, 134
Turgor pressure, 22, 134

Vacuoles, 20
Van Helmont, J.B., 12-13, 56
Vascular bundles, 135
    leaf structure and, 44, 45
    root structure and, 46-47, 77
    stem structure and, 40-41
    transport and, 86
Vascular cambium, 42, 135
Veins. *See* Vascular bundles
Vesicles, 91, 135
Vesicular-arbuscular mycorrhizae (VAM), 91-93, 128

Water
    bound, 65, 126
    free, 65, 129
    phloem and, 85-87
    photosynthesis and, 48-49
    stomata and, 43-45
    transport and, 80, 83
    xylem and, 41, 42, 84-85
Water lilies, 45
Water potential, 79, 83, 135
Water swelling capacity, 66-69, 135
Wax, 40, 43, 46

Xylem, 40-42, 44, 46-47, 82, 84-87

Yields, 53, 119-120

Zinc, 34, 87, 95
Zone of cell division, elongation, and maturation, 77, 135

142

page:

About the Author

Alex C. Wiedenhoeft, a botanist with over 10 years of experience working in the field of structural plant anatomy, has authored several research papers, a graduate-level book chapter, and an identification manual. He has B.S. and M.S. degrees from the University of Wisconsin-Madison, Department of Botany, and serves as an associate editor for the *International Association of Wood Anatomists Journal*. He and his wife raise children and trees on a small property in southwestern Wisconsin, surrounded on all sides by everyday, practical examples of plant nutrition and industrialized agriculture.